D1707933

GENESIS to REVELATION

ISAIAH

LLOYD BAILEY

A Comprehensive Verse-by-Verse Exploration of the Bible

GENESIS to REVELATION

ISAIAH

LLOYD BAILEY

GENESIS TO REVELATION SERIES:
ISAIAH
PARTICIPANT

Copyright© 1983 by Graded Press
Revised Edition Copyright © 1997 by Abingdon Press
Updated and Revised Edition Copyright © 2019 by Abingdon Press
All rights reserved.

No part of this work may be reproduced or transmitted in any form or by any means, electronic or mechanical, including photocopying and recording, or by any information or retrieval system, except as may be expressly permitted in the 1976 Copyright Act or in writing from the publisher. Requests for permission should be addressed in writing to Permissions, The United Methodist Publishing House, 2222 Rosa L. Parks Blvd., Nashville, TN 37228-0988 or e-mailed to permissions@umpublishing.org.

All Scripture quotations, unless otherwise indicated, are taken from the Holy Bible, New International Version®, NIV®. Copyright ©1973, 1978, 1984, 2011 by Biblica, Inc.™ Used by permission of Zondervan. All rights reserved worldwide. www.zondervan.com The "NIV" and "New International Version" are trademarks registered in the United States Patent and Trademark Office by Biblica, Inc.™

Scripture quotations marked REB are from the Revised English Bible © Oxford University Press and Cambridge University Press 1989.

Scripture quotations marked (CEV) are from the Contemporary English Version Copyright © 1991, 1992, 1995 by American Bible Society, Used by Permission.

Scripture quotations marked (NRSV) are taken from the New Revised Standard Version of the Bible, copyright 1989, Division of Christian Education of the National Council of the Churches of Christ in the United States of America. Used by permission. All rights reserved.

Scripture quotations marked (NJB) are excerpts from THE NEW JERUSALEM BIBLE, copyright © 1985 by Darton, Longman & Todd, Ltd. and Doubleday, a division of Random House, Inc. Reprinted by Permission.

Scripture quotations marked (NAB) are taken from the *New American Bible with Revised New Testament and New Psalms* © 1991, 1986, 1970 Confraternity of Christian Doctrine, Washington, D.C. and are used by permission of the copyright owner. All Rights Reserved. No part of the *New American Bible* may be reproduced in any form without permission in writing from the copyright owner.

ISBN 9781501855665

Manufactured in the United States of America
19 20 21 22 23 24 25 26 27 28—10 9 8 7 6 5 4 3 2 1

ABINGDON PRESS
Nashville

TABLE OF CONTENTS

*See now, the Lord, / the Lord Almighty, / is about to take
from Jerusalem and Judah / both supply and support. (3:1)*

1

PROPHECIES AGAINST JUDAH

Isaiah 1–5

DIMENSION ONE:

WHAT DOES THE BIBLE SAY?

Answer these questions by reading Isaiah 1

1. How have the people's sins affected their relationship with God? (1:4)

2. What evidence of God's anger does the prophet cite? (1:7)

3. Why did anyone in the city of Jerusalem survive the invasion? (1:9)

4. Why is God offended by offerings? (1:13, 15)

5. What response does God desire? (1:16-17)

6. What will God finally do for the people? (1:26)

Answer these questions by reading Isaiah 2

7. How are the contents of this chapter described? (2:1)

8. When will the prophet's expectations for the future be fulfilled? (2:2)

9. What are the expressions of time? (These expressions indicate a new topic or a new audience.) (2:2, 12, 20)

10. Why has God rejected the house of Jacob? (2:8, 18, 20)

11. What will God do to the proud? (2:11, 12)

Answer these questions by reading Isaiah 3

12. In what order are the country and capital city mentioned, compared to their order in 1:1 and 2:1? (3:1, 8)

13. Who is the speaker in verses 1-5? (3:4)

14. Who is the speaker in verses 6-8? (3:8)

15. What justification does the prophet give for the punishment of his society? (3:8-9)

16. What key words are repeated to give the chapter unity? (3:4, 6, 12, 14)

Answer these questions by reading Isaiah 4

17. What group of persons is discussed here? (4:1)

18. What introductory phrase is common to both verses 1 and 2? (4:2; see also 2:20; 3: 18)

19. What does God want to happen? (4:3-4)

Answer these questions by reading Isaiah 5

20. What is the basic complaint concerning the vineyard? (5:2)

21. What action will the owner of the vineyard now take? (5:5-6)

22. What does the vineyard represent in this parable? (5:7)

23. What phrase is used to in traduce the sections that follow? (5:8, 11, 18)

DIMENSION TWO: WHAT DOES THE BIBLE MEAN?

■ **Background.** Chapters 1–5 have a topical similarity, and may be called "Prophecies Against Judah." The prophet's speeches have been brought together to balance negative, judgmental sections with positive, hopeful ones. The positive speeches are 2:2-4 and 4:2-6. The entire section ends on a negative note (chap. 5). The collection appears to begin at 2:1. Chapter 1 was probably added as an introduction to the entire book when the "Prophecies Against Judah" were combined with other speeches.

■ **Isaiah 1.** The chapter has the following parts: introductory heading (v. 1), a word to survivors of a Judean national crisis (vv. 2-9), commentary on contemporary worship (vv. 10-20), and God's redemptive judgment (vv. 21-31). Within these sections, there may be other small divisions.

■ **Isaiah 1:2.** The appeal to the heavens and earth to hear the Lord's complaint against the people is a concept borrowed from international diplomacy and from the courts of law. Treaties and covenants between humans must be witnessed, so an agreement between God and people was said to be witnessed by "heavens" and "earth." Those witnesses are now called to testify to the rightness of God's cause. This analogy reveals the covenant background from which the prophet spoke.

■ **Isaiah 1:3-4.** What the people fail to know and understand is how gracious God has been to them in the past. Gratitude for God's generosity should now be translated into ethics. But their present activities make it clear how utterly estranged from that covenant concept the people have become (v. 4).

God's holiness will not allow the people to continue their sinful acts indefinitely. Such acts are in violation of a promise of fidelity the people made to the Holy One when they accepted the covenant.

- **Isaiah 1:7-9.** The prophet refers to an invasion of the country in the year 701 BC, when only the capital city and the Temple area (Zion) escaped destruction.
- **Isaiah 1:9.** The invasion is not presented solely as an instance of divine judgment for the people's sins. The narrow escape is attributed to God's continued and unmerited graciousness ("The Lord . . . left us some survivors"). The realization of such graciousness ought to stimulate the people to change their priorities and repent.
- **Isaiah 1:10-20.** God is not pleased with rituals and sacrifice unless the worshiper also follows the laws that are part of the covenant. Note the expressions "meaningless offerings" and "worthless assemblies" (v. 13). The prophet is issuing, not a blanket rejection of the sacrificial system, but rejection of the rituals that are not accompanied by covenant obedience.
- **Isaiah 1:16.** The prophet refers to a ritual act that took place during the festival at which he was speaking. He suggests that the washing ought to be more than physical.
- **Isaiah 1:18-20.** God is still gracious. The future is still open, if the people will only respond in an appropriate way.
- **Isaiah 1:21-31.** The contrast between past and present in Jerusalem's religious life is dealt with here. The city, once faithful, has become degenerate, just as metal, mixed with impurities or water, becomes contaminated. God, compared to a metallurgist, will purge the society and restore to it its former condition.
- **Isaiah 1:29.** The worship of fertility deities was often carried out in sacred groves or gardens. Such activity has contributed to the people's estrangement from the Lord. Worship of these deities was thought to ensure the renewal of nature in the springtime. But in Israel's case, rather than a renewal, it will lead to withering destruction.
- **Isaiah 2.** This chapter has the following sections: an editorial introduction (v. 1), the goal of history (vv. 2-4), a personal word of exhortation (v. 5), three speeches

condemning pride and idolatry (vv. 6-11, 12-19, 20-21), and a final exhortation (v. 22).

■ **Isaiah 2:6-21.** Three speeches that were delivered at different times and places seem to have been combined here (vv. 6-11, 12-19, 20-21). They may be read and appreciated independently, without searching for an overall progression of thought. Notice how certain themes or expressions tend to be repeated in each section. This repetition suggests a thematic collection.

■ **Isaiah 3.** This chapter is made up of a series of speeches about the coming chaos in Judah and its causes. Note that some parts are poetry and some prose.

■ **Isaiah 3:4.** The leaders of the country will be so thoroughly destroyed that only the inexperienced (boys and children) will be available to take their places.

■ **Isaiah 3:16–4:1.** The women of the city are a new object of the prophet's criticism. This section seems to be made up of a series of once-independent criticisms. Prose and poetry are alternated. The section also contains introductory phrases such as "in that day." This section may have been joined to the larger context because of the theme of human pride (vv. 8, 16), and because women are mentioned in verse 12. The attack is not on dress itself, but on the preoccupation with dress to the exclusion of traditional religious values. This concern for clothing is merely a symptom of a deeper spiritual sickness.

■ **Isaiah 4:5.** "Cloud of smoke by day and a glow of flaming fire by night" is an allusion to Exodus 13:21-22, where these objects symbolized God's presence during the desert journey. Those temporary signs will now be made permanent, an enduring sense of the divine presence. The same idea is conveyed by saying that the pavilion that accompanied the people in the desert (Exodus 40) will be a permanent fixture. The Book of Revelation uses a related image to reaffirm the divine presence: a "new Jerusalem" will descend from heaven (Revelation 21:1-4).

- **Isaiah 5.** This material may be divided into the parable of the vineyard (vv. 1-7), a series of "woe prophecies" condemning certain groups, and an outline of the resulting punishment (vv. 8-30).
- **Isaiah 5:1-7.** The parable has four stanzas, and the concluding one contains the interpretation (v. 7).
- **Isaiah 5:7.** The difference between the expected harvest and the wild grapes is translated into social terms by means of a pun that is lost in translation.
- **Isaiah 5:8-23.** The series of criticisms (introduced by "Woe to . . .") serves to illustrate the injustices in Judean society that may be compared with wild grapes.
- **Isaiah 5:8-10.** Accumulation of the real estate of others was frowned upon in Israel's sacred literature. This action fostered economic classes and inequality. It also was an arrogant assertion that humans were the absolute owners of land. By contrast, the ancient Israelites believed that land belonged to God. God graciously loaned it to the people (Leviticus 25). God's gift could not be taken away by someone else. The prophet says that the entire land will be taken away (the people will be exiled), and agriculture will fail as punishment for violating this ancient principle. It is especially appropriate that vineyards fail, in view of the previous parable of the vineyard. The prophet's disciples may have placed this woe (vv. 8-10) first in the sequence of "woes" for just this reason.
- **Isaiah 5:11-17.** The activities of the rich are not so wrong themselves. But they divert attention from traditional religious values. Just as appetites are insatiable, so are the forces of destruction ("Death"). Jerusalem will become a heap of ruins (v. 17), a theme in keeping with the parable in verses 1-7.
- **Isaiah 5:18-19.** Some people have become so callous in their disregard for the faith that they respond with arrogant mockery to anyone who reminds them of it. They say, in effect, "We challenge God to act, if God exists!"

■ **Isaiah 5:20-21.** These two woes denounce those who are clever enough to rationalize their base behavior until it appears justified ("those who call evil good"). In doing so, they deceive themselves, since they are clever only in their own eyes. In contrast, Israel's truly wise people assert that wisdom begins with reverence for the Lord (Proverbs 1:7).

DIMENSION THREE: WHAT DOES THE BIBLE MEAN TO ME?

Isaiah 1:2-4—The Ingratitude of the Blessed

Israel's ancient traditions suggested that, although God had chosen and blessed the people, this need not have happened. Such actions were undeserved and should have generated a sense of gratitude in the people. This gratitude should be expressed in specific acts of obedience to God and in responsibility for others. Thus the prophets can accuse the people of more than the commission of wrong acts. The people are guilty of ingratitude and rebellion as well.

What gracious acts have been accorded the people of God throughout history? How is gratitude to God being expressed by the church (your church) today? How can the church better express gratitude to God? Can you cite instances of failure?

Isaiah 2:2-4—A Golden Age

The prophet has expressed the belief that the world need not remain as it is. Rather, he believes that God is working to bring about an ideal age "in the last days" (v. 2). Do you think the world has progressed toward the ideal since the time of Isaiah? Can you cite instances of success? Regressions? Is such a belief realistic? Do you believe it and strive toward it? What groups now are working toward that goal? Are they overtly religious groups?

Isaiah 5:1-7—God's Expectations of the Community

The prophet is struck by the vast gap between God's expectations for the people and the present reality. He believes that God has but one course of action if the situation is to be remedied. The people must be exiled to a foreign land. How can this episode be a model for understanding the present and future of the church? Is the church more obedient now than ancient Israel was? Is God more tolerant of the church's betrayals than of those in ancient Judah? Could the church be punished to the extreme that the ancient community was? What events today might be interpreted as God's judgment on the church? Could the church even be rejected? Could God start anew?

In the year that King Uzziah died, I saw the Lord, high and exalted, seated on a throne; and the train of his robe filled the temple. (6:1)

THE CALL OF ISAIAH

Isaiah 6–12

DIMENSION ONE: WHAT DOES THE BIBLE SAY?

Answer these questions by reading Isaiah 6

1. Where was the prophet when he had this religious experience? (6:1)

2. What was the prophet's response when he sensed the divine presence? (6:5)

3. How is God described? (6:1, 5)

4. What was the prophet commissioned to do? (6:10)

Answer these questions by reading Isaiah 7

5. What crisis set the stage for this chapter? (7:1, 2, 4)

6: What evidence is there that someone else besides Isaiah is the storyteller now? (7:3)

7. Who have King Ahaz's enemies threatened to put on the throne of Judah? (7:6)

8. Does the prophet think Ahaz's enemies will succeed? (7:7-8)

9. For whom is the sign intended? (7:14)

10. How old will the boy be when Ahaz's enemies are defeated? (7:16)

11. What foreign power will take possession of Judah if the prophet's advice is not followed? (7:17)

Answer these questions by reading Isaiah 8

12. What foreign powers continue to threaten King Ahaz of Judah? (8:4)

13. What does the prophet think will happen if the leaders of Judah refuse to listen? (8:7-8)

14. Was Isaiah a solitary individual, or did he have followers? (8:16)

15. Who do the people turn to for guidance in the crisis? (8:19)

Answer these questions by reading Isaiah 9

16. What parts of Israel have already fallen under Assyrian power? (9:1)

17. Where will the deliverer live, and over what will he rule? (9:7)

18. What phrase concludes each of several short speeches? (9:12, 17, 21; 10:4)

Answer these questions by reading Isaiah 10

19. For what sin will the Assyrians be punished? (10:12)

20. What does the prophet hope will finally happen? (10:21)

Answer these questions by reading Isaiah 11

21. With what image does this chapter begin? (11:1)

22. Rather than trust in his own power as Ahaz seems to have done, what will guide the new ruler? (11:2-3)

Answer this question by reading Isaiah 12

23. What is the people's attitude toward God now? (12:2)

DIMENSION TWO: WHAT DOES THE BIBLE MEAN?

■ **Background.** Chapters 6–12 begin with Isaiah's summons to be a prophet. These chapters, written in prose, are concerned primarily with a major political crisis. The entire section may be described as "The Call of Isaiah."

■ **Isaiah 6:1.** King Uzziah's death signals the beginning of a time of uncertainty about the nation's future. The Assyrians had recently begun an aggressive expansion into Syria and Palestine, but King Uzziah was able to forge alliances that held them at bay. Isaiah, as he worships in the Temple, expresses his experience of God's presence and control in political terms. That is, he interprets it in a way that is relevant for the present.

■ **Isaiah 6:2.** The word *feet* is a common euphemism for genitals.

■ **Isaiah 6:3.** The repetition of words in the Hebrew language is a way of expressing emphasis. That "the whole earth is full of [God's] glory" means that all events are under divine control. Thus Uzziah's death need not be an occasion for despair.

■ **Isaiah 6:5.** Isaiah feels unworthy to exist. He feels God owes him nothing, not even life. His *lips* are mentioned, not because he has indulged in loose talk, but as a figure of speech where the part stands for the whole person.

■ **Isaiah 6:6-7.** Isaiah can do nothing to remedy his status before God. Help can come only by an act of divine grace.

■ **Isaiah 6:9-10.** The prophet's message, in accordance with God's wish, will provoke the people. Rather than repent, they will become even more stubborn and entrenched in their values and actions. This attitude will hasten the divine judgment.

■ **Isaiah 6:11-13.** The nature and extent of the judgment now becomes clear. An invasion and destruction will occur at the hands of foreigners.

■ **Isaiah 6:13.** Note that the prophet's commission, beginning at verse 9, ends one line short of the end of the chapter. The remaining line "But as the terebinth . . ." entirely changes the meaning of the passage. The prophet has used the word *stump* in a negative sense. Even those Judeans who survive the Assyrian attack will be destroyed, much as a stump is burned when shoots come up again. But the last line transforms the stump into a positive image. Life will survive in it, despite all destructive efforts. This line was probably added later. The prophet elsewhere has expressed a belief that a remnant would survive to form a new community (see the text note to Isaiah 7:3; see also 11:1). The "holy seed" is that surviving, righteous remnant.

■ **Isaiah 7:2.** The rulers of Syria and Israel, fearful of an attack by the Assyrians, try to forge a new alliance to keep them at bay. *Ephraim*, the largest tribe in the Northern Kingdom, is sometimes used as a synonym for *Israel*.

■ **Isaiah 7:3-6.** If Ahaz joins the alliance and it fails, Judah will be destroyed by the Assyrians. If he does not join it, the alliance will replace him with Tabeel, who favors their strategy. If he asks the Assyrians for help, he must become their vassal, and Judah's independence will be lost.

■ **Isaiah 7:7-9.** Isaiah advises Ahaz to do nothing. The enemies will soon be defeated. The "it" that will not come to pass is the alliance and its plans.

■ **Isaiah 7:8.** The word *for* obscures the meaning here. The Hebrew word can also be translated *that*. What is it that will not endure as a threat to Ahaz: Damascus as the head of Syria (Aram) and Rezin as king of Damascus!

■ **Isaiah 7:10-11.** These verses tell us that the king does not take Isaiah's advice. Ahaz explains that he will not test the Lord, as Isaiah has advised. As a matter of fact, however, the king may already have decided to ask the Assyrians to help, which he did (2 Kings 16:1-9).

■ **Isaiah 7:14.** This sign has an entirely different purpose than the one the king has just refused to request. It will not determine foreign policy by convincing the king that Isaiah is giving him sound advice. Rather, it will serve to remind the king, once the crisis is over, that the prophet spoke the truth. Every time the king sees Immanuel, the king will be reminded that God was with the people in the crisis with the alliance, just as Isaiah had said! The child is likely the prophet's own son. He gave symbolic names to his other children during this same crisis (7:3; 8:3). The mother might be either the prophetess (8:3) or some other wife. The Hebrew word translated as *virgin*, is *almah*, which indicates a young woman.

■ **Isaiah 7:15.** "Curds and honey" may mean that things will go well. Ahaz's policy will seem to have been a wise one.

■ **Isaiah 7:17.** The prophet continues in a positive vein until the last clause. The days of curds and honey are a prelude to disaster. The Assyrians will be, not the saviors that Ahaz thought they were, but destroyers.

■ **Isaiah 7:18-25.** This section contains a series of reflections on the future Assyrian presence in Judah. Each reflection begins with the traditional formula of introduction, "In that day . . ." (meaning "in days to come").

■ **Isaiah 7:18-19.** The image of a fly or bee may have been used because those on whom they swarm are defenseless.

■ **Isaiah 7:20.** Conquerors sometimes stripped captives and shaved them as a sign of dishonor (see comment on 6:2).

■ **Isaiah 7:21.** The standard of living will be reduced to the lowest level. No one will have more than one or two animals. Only by that narrow margin will they escape starvation.

■ **Isaiah 7:22.** This verse seems to promise abundance. Will those left in the land be fortunate compared to those slain or taken into exile?

■ **Isaiah 8.** This chapter can be read in four sections. In verses 1-4, the prophet gives his son a symbolic name in anticipation of Judah's deliverance from the alliance. In verses 5-8, Isaiah's response to the king's failure to take his advice reflects the same tone as 7:10-17. Verses 9-10 reflect the optimistic period of 7:7-8 and 8:1-4. Verses 11-22 contain Isaiah's private reflections to his disciples after Ahaz rejects his advice.

■ **Isaiah 8:3.** The "prophetess" (Isaiah's wife) may be the same woman as the young woman of 7:14. The events seem parallel.

■ **Isaiah 8:6.** The waters of Shiloah are Jerusalem's water supply. They symbolize the life-giving advice that God has offered through the prophet.

■ **Isaiah 8:7.** The Euphrates River marks a boundary of the Assyrian Empire. In these verses, the river symbolizes Assyria's power, as it does in 7:20. The Judeans, through their king, have chosen a raging and destructive river rather than a life-giving spring.

■ **Isaiah 8:8.** The comforting name *Immanuel* (meaning "God is with us") is now used sarcastically.

■ **Isaiah 8:11-15.** The prophet, disappointed that Ahaz has chosen to rely on the Assyrians rather than to trust the Lord, temporarily withdraws from public life. He now reflects on the situation in the presence of a small group of followers.

■ **Isaiah 8:14-15.** The people, having rejected God's advice and offer of deliverance (8:5), will not find security. Having stumbled in their faith, they must suffer the consequences.

■ **Isaiah 8:16-18.** Isaiah wants the people to know, in the difficult days ahead, that they had been offered an alternative. Isaiah's words and actions, including the names of his children, now serve as testimony to that fact. His disciples witness the fact that his warnings were delivered in advance, just as he claims.

■ **Isaiah 8:19-22.** In a crisis, occult practices appeal to the people as a way to learn the future. Superstition cannot produce a new dawn for the people, and will only further the coming of exile.

■ **Isaiah 9:1.** In response to the alliance that formed against him (see note on 7:2), the king of Assyria has attacked and added part of Israel to his empire. The conquered areas were Galilee (Zebulun and Naphtali), the coastal plain ("the Way of the Sea"), and the land beyond the Jordan. Isaiah believes their present gloom will end when God (the unexplained "he" in the passage) graciously acts on their behalf.

■ **Isaiah 9:2.** In this section (vv. 1-7), Isaiah expects a new era beyond the period of Assyrian domination. Although the expected deliverance lies in the not-too-distant future, the prophet describes it in the past tense. Isaiah also believes the deliverer may already have been born (v. 6).

■ **Isaiah 9:4.** The words *yoke*, *bar*, and *rod* all refer to the Assyrian oppressors. They will be expelled, just as the invading Midianites were cast out long ago (Judges 6:1–8:28).

■ **Isaiah 9:6-7.** The era of restoration will take place under the leadership of a prince of the Davidic line. Isaiah's song may have been composed in celebration of that prince's birth and in anticipation of his accomplishments.

■ **Isaiah 9:6.** Kings in the ancient Near East were often said to be godlike, and liked being addressed as "god." That a Judean king is described here in such terms is not surprising.

■ **Isaiah 9:8-21.** We now return to the condemnation of the people for the pride and wickedness that characterized chapters 1–5.

■ **Isaiah 9:8-9.** *Jacob* and *Israel* are equivalent terms in parallel poetic lines. Ephraim is the predominant tribe. Samaria is the capital city.

■ **Isaiah 9:10.** The people, rather than heeding the prophet's warnings, become more determined to continue their traditional ways. This response illustrates the prophet's commission in 6:10. Preaching to them will have a negative effect.

▪ **Isaiah 9:14.** This verse probably refers to the revolution that ended the reign of Ahab and Jezebel (2 Kings 9–10).

▪ **Isaiah 10.** This complex chapter may be divided into five sections: verses 1-4 continue the collection of paragraphs that began at 9:8, each ending with "his hand is still upraised." The next section is a commentary on the pride of the Assyrian conquerors (vv. 5-19). The third section is an expectation that the exiled Israelites will return (vv. 20-27). Verses 28-32 describe the Assyrian advance against Jerusalem in 701 BC. The final section deals with the consequences of the Assyrian attack (vv. 33-34).

▪ **Isaiah 10:1-4.** All previous means of communicating with the people of Judah have failed. They have not learned the lessons of history, and now divine judgment will fall (v. 4).

▪ **Isaiah 10:9.** Various places the Assyrian army has captured are cited, and they now approach Judah. Following their conquest of areas of Israel in 734–733 BC, they destroyed the capital city (Samaria) in 721. They exiled large elements of the population (2 Kings 17:1-6). Judah was spared because of King Ahaz's pro-Assyrian policy. However, his successor, King Hezekiah, tried to restore Judean independence from Assyria. Judah ultimately was invaded.

▪ **Isaiah 10:16.** This verse seems to reflect the fact that the Assyrian army withdrew from the siege of Jerusalem in 701 BC.

▪ **Isaiah 10:16-17.** Repeated use of the pronoun *he* can create confusion here: "his sturdy warriors," "his pomp," and "his thorns and his briers" refer to the king of Assyria. "Their Holy One" refers to God, here called the "Light of Israel."

▪ **Isaiah 10:22.** The purpose of the destruction that God has brought through the Assyrians is to produce a righteous remnant. God's judgment is ultimately redemptive.

■ **Isaiah 10:24-27.** The tone of this section is so positive that it contrasts with much of Isaiah's previous message. The audience is addressed warmly, rather than as totally wicked (1:4). The Assyrians are presented as the enemies of God. They are not God's chosen instrument to punish a deserving Judah (5:26-30; 6:11-12; 7:18-25). This section was probably composed by Isaiah's disciples. They knew that the Assyrians withdrew in 701 BC. Perhaps they wanted to remember the prophet only in a positive and supportive light.

■ **Isaiah 10:28-32.** The Assyrian advance (701 BC) is graphically described. "They," in verses 28-29, are the forces of Sennacherib, king of Assyria.

■ **Isaiah 10:33-34.** Presumably, these verses describe the results of the Assyrian advance outlined in 10:28-32. Lebanon (Syria and Palestine) and Judah will be cut down by the invading Assyrians as easily as foresters cut down trees.

■ **Isaiah 11.** Chapter 11 deals with the expectation of a new era under the leadership of a righteous member of the royal house, and the return of the people from their exile (vv. 10-16).

■ **Isaiah 11:1.** Jesse was the father of David, so the verse is referring to the traditional royal family. Only when the tree is cut down can a new, vigorous shoot come forth.

■ **Isaiah 11:2-5.** This ruler will rely on God rather than on his own schemes. He will be what God wanted human leadership to be when the monarchy was first instituted.

■ **Isaiah 11:6-9.** The recovery of the harmonious world God intended at creation is described in poetic language.

■ **Isaiah 12.** This chapter is a song of praise. The congregation confesses that God's judgment has been merited and was ultimately redemptive.

DIMENSION THREE: WHAT DOES THE BIBLE MEAN TO ME?

Isaiah 6:9-13—How Is Success to Be Measured?

Has the prophet been commissioned by God to be a failure? What is it, positively, that he is to try to accomplish? Is the prophetic task different from the ministerial task today? How is the prophet's strange mission similar to a minister's task today? Which ministers are successful in the public mind? Why?

Isaiah 7:14—The Old Testament in the New

This verse is cited in the New Testament in connection with the birth of Jesus (Matthew 1:23). Specifically, what use does Matthew make of Isaiah 7:14? Which of the following do you think is most nearly correct? (1) What Isaiah meant is clarified by the New Testament. Matthew 1:23 is the inspired translation of the prophet. The prophet has been able to see far into the future and predict the birth of Jesus. (2) What Isaiah meant is clarified by reading his words in their literary and historical context. He referred to a child in his own time, and Matthew misunderstood him. (3) Matthew is drawing a parallel, not predicting. Just as God gave a sign then—that God is with us—God gives a sign now. Use of the word *fulfill* (Matthew 1:22) need not mean "to make a prediction come true."

Isaiah 8:19-20—The Prophet and Mediums

When, in times of crisis in the Bible, have people turned to wizards and mediums to learn about the future? Do you know, or know of, persons who claim to have the ability to contact the dead? What is your opinion of this practice? What does the prophet seem to regard as the only legitimate source of knowledge of the supernatural? Which of the following do you think is more nearly correct? (1) The Bible means that people can actually do such things, but the faithful should not participate in them. (2) The Bible merely describes people who claim to do such things. It does not necessarily acknowledge that they are successful.

Isaiah 10:33–11:1—How to Effect a Change of Heart

The prophet calls for repentance—a genuine, enduring change of heart or of priorities. What are some shallow motives for change, which might have been at work until God took drastic measures? When have you repented out of fear, or because it appeared to be the smart thing to do under the circumstances? Did that repentance "stick" to effect true change, or did you revert to comfortable behavior when the circumstances changed? Do persons, or even institutions, usually reform spontaneously? Is some pressure necessary to bring about change? Are God's judgment and grace opposite sides of God, or are they really "two sides of the same coin"? When have you seen both these elements at work at the same time?

Babylon, the jewel of kingdoms, / the pride and glory of the Babylonians, / will be overthrown by God / like Sodom and Gomorrah. (13:19)

PROPHECIES AGAINST THE ENEMIES

Isaiah 13–17

DIMENSION ONE: WHAT DOES THE BIBLE SAY?

Answer these questions by reading Isaiah 13

1. How is this new material described? (13:1)

2. Who is warning of impending battle? (13:2-4)

3. Who are the conquerors from faraway lands? (13:4, 17)

4. Against what specific city is this prophecy directed? (13:1, 19)

Answer these questions by reading Isaiah 14

5. What will the Lord do for Israel? (14:1)

6. Against whom is the taunt in verses 4-21 directed? (14:4)

7. What world power does the Bible mention in verses 24-27? (14:25)

Answer these questions by reading Isaiah 15

8. What is the prophet's response to the tragedy in Moab? (15:5)

9. What is the nature of the catastrophe that has struck Moab? (15:4, 9)

Answer these questions by reading Isaiah 16

10. From whom do refugees from Moab seek help? (16:1)

11. How is Moab answered? (16:6-7)

12. Is the entire chapter spoken at the same time, or were additions made to it at a later time? (16:13-14)

Answer these questions by reading Isaiah 17

13. What enemies of Judah are denounced here? (17:3)

14. What consequences of the divine judgment does the writer expect? (17:7)

DIMENSION TWO: WHAT DOES THE BIBLE MEAN?

■ **Background.** Chapters 13–23 are a self-contained booklet within the larger Book of Isaiah. Basically a collection of poems against Judah's neighbors, the poems are introduced as prophecies (13:1; 14:28; 15:1; 17:1; 19:1; 21:1, 11, 13; 22:1; 23:1).

Isaiah probably did not write this section himself; it reflects a differing point of view from the previous sections. Parts of it seem to have knowledge of events that happened long after Isaiah's death. Generations of the prophet's followers must have contributed to both the organization and the contents.

■ **Isaiah 13:1.** Babylonia, whose capital city was Babylon, was part of the Assyrian Empire until it became independent about 625 BC. Thus Babylonia posed no threat to Judah until about 650 BC, long after the time of Isaiah (whose dates are perhaps 780–760 BC). The writer's longing for Babylon's destruction may even mean that he lived at a time when that power had control of his country (586–538 BC).

■ **Isaiah 13:2.** Someone (perhaps an army leader) is commanded to signal for the mobilization of his troops. They are to attack Babylon through its main gate.

■ **Isaiah 13:3.** The "I" who issued the command is the Lord.

■ **Isaiah 13:4-16.** In this section, divine anger seems directed at the entire world, as opposed to Babylonia alone.

■ **Isaiah 13:6.** "The day of the LORD" is a time that Israel's prophets expected in the near future, when Israel and Judah would forsake evil and worship the true God.

■ **Isaiah 13:14.** The description shifts here from punishment of the world through the anger of the Lord to slaughter of a particular, unnamed place (probably Babylon, as in v. 1).

■ **Isaiah 13:17.** This verse enables us to date the time of the speaker fairly precisely. He knows that the Medes (from northern Iran) did not begin to move westward and pose a threat to nations there until about 620 BC.

■ **Isaiah 14.** This complex chapter has three sections. Verses 1-23 are a taunt song against the king of Babylon, with a prose preface and conclusion. Verses 24-27 deal with deliverance from Assyrian domination. Verses 28-32 contain a warning to the Philistines and assurances to Judah (Zion).

■ **Isaiah 14:1-3.** That many Judeans have been exiled to Babylon at the time of this writer is suggested by the following language: "Once again he will choose Israel" and "bring them to their own place" (see comment on 13:1).

■ **Isaiah 14:9.** In ancient Near Eastern belief, a faint remnant of each person (a shade) descends to Sheol to reside forever. Sheol is not a place of punishment. The NIV consistently translates Sheol as "the grave" (v. 11) or "the realm of the dead" (vv. 9, 15). The point here is that the king of Babylon meets the same end as any other mortal.

■ **Isaiah 14:12.** The text continues to speak of the king of Babylon, contrasting the power of his former life with his powerlessness in the face of death. Whereas he may have been addressed by such flattering titles as "morning star, son of the dawn," now he ends up as nothing more than a "corpse" (v. 19).

■ **Isaiah 14:17.** This Babylonian king has refused to release the Judean captives. The Exile lasted for decades (586–538 BC). The king is condemned for his pride and self-reliance, a theme the prophet has treated before (10:7-19).

■ **Isaiah 14:24-27.** When we move from verse 23 (about Babylonian domination) to verse 24 (about Assyrian domination), we jump backward in time from the sixth to the eighth century BC. This move illustrates how the prophet's disciples joined various prophecies to speak to the needs of the times.

■ **Isaiah 14:29.** The word *rod* presumably refers to the king of Assyria. His death has produced hope for deliverance and independence among the cities on the coast of Palestine.

The king might be Sargon, who died in 705 BC. The prophet anticipates that his successors (the "viper" and the "venomous serpent") will be even more oppressive than he was.

■ **Isaiah 14:30-32.** The ideas of continued oppression of Philistia and contrasting security for Judah are presented here. The two topics seem scrambled, and will be clearer if read in the following verse sequence: 29, 31, 30, 32.

■ **Isaiah 14:30.** The poor and needy seem to be Judah.

■ **Isaiah 15:1–16:11.** This anti-Moab passage is difficult to interpret. Nonetheless, it does have a thematic unity. But note the switch from poetry to prose in 16:13-14, which may signal another author or situation. Verse 13 clarifies this passage by reflecting on the material that comes before it.

■ **Isaiah 15:1.** Ar is sometimes a synonym for Moab. Kir may be the capital city.

■ **Isaiah 15:2.** Shaving was a traditional sign of mourning.

■ **Isaiah 15:5.** The poet apparently gives his reaction to the scene, or to a report of the scene.

■ **Isaiah 15:9.** Apparently, God now speaks. The Moabites have not gotten all that they deserve. The crisis is not over.

■ **Isaiah 16:1.** The rulers of Moab have sent gifts to the ruler of Judah ("the land"). This action signals submission and indicates the desire for protection from the invaders described in chapter 15.

■ **Isaiah 16:4-5.** In mid-verse, there is a sudden transition. Beginning with "The oppressor . . .," the verse speaks of Judah's future security, when its oppressor will be no more. The passage seems related in theme to 9:1-7; 10:24-27; 11:1-5. Here that theme has been placed inside the Moab prophecy. The message seems to be that the time will come when Judah can offer security and stability to its neighbors.

■ **Isaiah 16:6-11.** These verses answer the Moabites' entreaty, in the form of mocking lament.

■ **Isaiah 16:13-14.** By the time this section was added, Moab had recovered from the invasion of 15:1–16:11 and had become an enemy of Judah and presumably of God. A final word of judgment is pronounced concerning the Moabites. This brief prose section may reveal why the longer poem, about an event in the past, was preserved. God's action in the past provides the basis for hope in the future. Moab, having once been judged, is not immune from judgment again.

■ **Isaiah 17.** The verses in this chapter may be grouped as follows for easier reading: (1) destruction of the neighboring Syrians (Aramites) and Israelites (vv. 1-3); (2) divine displeasure with Israel in particular (vv. 4-6); (3) expectation of an age of true worship (vv. 7-8); (4) reasons for God's displeasure with Israel (vv. 9-11, apparently meant to continue the thought of vv. 4-6; and (5) the security of Zion in the face of enemy attack (vv. 12-14). Such a rapid shifting of images seems unlikely for the prophet within such a short time. Possibly Isaiah's prophecies were later collected and arranged by his disciples. In addition, the question of authorship is raised by the pro-Zion section of verses 12-14, which conflicts so strongly with Isaiah's words of unrelenting judgment upon Judah (5:1-7; 6:1-13; 7:18-25).

■ **Isaiah 17:1.** Damascus is the capital of Syria.

■ **Isaiah 17:3.** The linking of Syria and Ephraim reminds us of the alliance of those two powers against Judah in chapter 7. Perhaps the present prophecy is from the same period.

■ **Isaiah 17:4-6.** The image seems to be that of exile, with only a few remnants of the former society left intact. After the alliance (17:3) failed to halt the Assyrian advance, the latter group captured northern Israel in 734–733 BC (9:1), and then the whole country in 721 BC (see comment on 10:9).

■ **Isaiah 17:8.** The Asherah poles are symbols for a Canaanite goddess of fertility.

■ **Isaiah 17:9.** The word *their* refers to the Israelites ("Jacob" in vv. 4-6). Just as the Hivites and Amorites were removed from the land at the time of Joshua, so will the present sinful inhabitants be removed.

33

■ **Isaiah 17:10-11.** In fertility cults, the return of the deity from the dead was celebrated by cultivating young plants.

■ **Isaiah 17:12-13.** The language used here is similar to that used in passages elsewhere that seem to be later than the time of the prophet (see, for example, 13:4-5).

DIMENSION THREE: WHAT DOES THE BIBLE MEAN TO ME?

Authorship and the Value of the Text

Some sections of this collection seem to describe events long after the lifetime of Isaiah; they reflect different attitudes toward Judah and the surrounding nations. Some scholars think the prophet's disciples not only edited his speeches, but expanded them with reflections of their own. How does that possibility raise problems for your faith in the Bible? Is the identification of the author important ("I trust Isaiah more than his followers")? Why, or why not? What is crucial for us as interpreters of the Bible: what is said or who said it? Can members of the community differ on authorship and authority, and yet remain faithful to the Scripture as written? Can those who disagree remain responsible members of the community?

When have you experienced division over the question of authorship, with one side condemning the other for having bad faith? Are there sections of the Bible, even books, for which no author is even proposed? If so, are these portions of Scripture less authoritative than those for whom the author is named? Why do you think that biblical stories or speeches were preserved in the first place?

Historical Correctness and the Value of the Text

In chapter 13, the author anticipates the destruction of the Babylonian Empire and then suggests how its end will come. Babylonia will end at the hand of the Medes, who will so destroy it that the city of Babylon "will never be inhabited" (v. 20). But in fact, the Medes and Babylonians became allies rather than enemies. Moreover, the Medes, rather than defeating Babylon, were themselves defeated by the neighboring Persians around 550 BC. Even then, Babylon remained a flourishing and heavily populated city. Babylon was even considered by Alexander the Great for the capital of his empire (about 325 BC). Under his successors, it declined in importance until it was sparsely inhabited by the time of Christianity.

How do you react to the fact that the writer of Isaiah 13 misjudged how Babylon would be defeated and that its defeat did not lead to its becoming uninhabited? Which of the following do you think is the most adequate evaluation? (1) The author, as a prophet, cannot be wrong. There must be some error in our understanding of the passage or of history. If we only understood more, we would see that the prophet was not in error. (2) The author was wrong. The Bible specifically says the Medes, not the Persians, will destroy the city, and that it will *then* be forever uninhabited, not some hundreds of years later. This means that the Bible is a fallible, human document. (3) The author is concerned with the future of the people of God. They have not been abandoned to the world empires, but will be restored and be God's servants. That message is the central faith that should be singled out for us, even if the writer could not correctly anticipate how and when it would come about. The writer's errors may be confessed without embarrassment. They do not detract from the truth of God's involvement in history.

Isaiah 14:24-27—Reinterpretation Within Scripture?

The writer proposes that the Assyrians will be expelled from Judah because of their military excesses and their pride. Presumably, then, the passage is a reaction to the events of 701 BC, when a massive invasion took place.

This message of hope clearly would have been preserved during the time of Assyrian control of Judah (which may have continued until well after the death of the prophet). But why would the message have been preserved after the Assyrians vanished from the international scene? (They were defeated by the Medes and Babylonians in 614–612 BC). Was the prophecy preserved primarily as a reminder of the prophet's accuracy in describing what happened back then? Or was it preserved because it was given a new meaning and made to speak to a new situation?

If the original code now speaks to a new situation, does it, therefore, have two meanings: (1) what the prophet intended, and (2) how the followers applied the prophecy? Is the original meaning more important than its new meaning? Are both meanings Scripture and equally valid? Which meaning speaks to the church today? How do we reapply Scripture to new situations today?

I will hand the Egyptians over / to the power of a cruel master, / and a fierce king will rule over them. (19:4)

PROPHECIES AGAINST EGYPT
Isaiah 18–23

DIMENSION ONE: WHAT DOES THE BIBLE SAY?

Answer these questions by reading Isaiah 18

1. Who will punish the Egyptians? (18:4-5)

2. Who are the "people tall and smooth-skinned" who will finally acknowledge the true God? (18:1-2, 7)

Answer these questions by reading Isaiah 19

3. What will happen to Egypt? (19:4)

4. What characteristic phrase, indicating a new composition, is found here? (19:16)

5. Why is the Lord punishing Egypt? (19:22)

Answer this question by reading Isaiah 20

6. In whom have the people of Palestine placed their hope of defeating the invading Assyrians? (20:5)

Answer these questions by reading Isaiah 21

7. Who are the nations of verse 2 attacking? (21:2, 9)

8. Why is domination by Babylonia being brought to an end? (21:2)

Answer these questions by reading Isaiah 22

9. What is the cause of the public rejoicing? (22:2-3)

10. What is the prophet's reaction to this same event? (22:4)

11. What public reaction should the situation have evoked rather than joy? (22:12)

Answer these questions by reading Isaiah 23

12. What caused the misfortune of Tyre? (23:8-9)

13. What fault of the city led to its destruction? (23:9, 12)

14. Against whom is most of the chapter directed? (23:2, 4, 12)

15. What is the ultimate fate of Tyre? (23:18)

DIMENSION TWO: WHAT DOES THE BIBLE MEAN?

■ **Background.** That chapters 13–23 of Isaiah belong together as a once-separate booklet was suggested at the beginning of Dimension Two of lesson 3. Chapters 13–23 may be divided into two sections: Chapters 13–17 are prophecies, primarily against Babylonia and other states to the north and east. Chapters 18–23 are prophecies, mainly against Egypt and other states to the south and west.

■ **Isaiah 18.** The chapter may be read as a unit, with the exception of verse 7. There, interest shifts from the imminent destruction of Egypt to an ideal future when Egypt will be subject to Judah and to the Lord.

■ **Isaiah 18:1.** Biblical Ethiopia is not the same area as modern Ethiopia. Rather, it is Cush, roughly equivalent to modern Sudan. Cushite monarchs invaded Egypt and ruled there during the period 725–663 BC. The words "whirring wings" may refer to swarms of locusts, for which Cush was well known.

■ **Isaiah 18:2.** The Cushites were known for their height and apparently for their relative lack of body hair. What the messengers are to announce to the rulers of Ethiopia (Cush, or Egypt) becomes clearer in verses 5-6.

■ **Isaiah 18:3.** A "banner" and "trumpet" may warn of war. This alerts us to the meaning of the verses that follow.

■ **Isaiah 18:5-6.** God will prune the nations just as a farmer prunes vines. The farmer is not improving the vines, but is removing troublesome sprouts. Presumably, Egypt is among them.

■ **Isaiah 18:7.** This verse seems to have a separate origin. Rather than condemning the Egyptians, it anticipates a time when they will join Judah in true worship. Similar in tone to 2:2-4 and 14:1-2, this verse was probably added to the original prophecy by a later generation of the prophet's followers.

■ **Isaiah 19.** Verses 1-15 contain a poem against Egypt, which may be divided into three stanzas (1-4, 5-10, 11-15). Verses 16-25 are prose additions to the poem, each introduced by the typical new beginning, "In that day." Whereas the poem is anti-Egyptian, the prose moves toward their conversion to true religion. It seems likely, then, that the prose comes from a later time than the poem.

■ **Isaiah 19:2.** A quotation of the Lord begins here and continues into verse 4.

■ **Isaiah 19:5-10.** The image shifts from civil chaos (vv. 1-4) to a debilitating drought. Scholars have often debated whether these two stanzas are by the same author.

■ **Isaiah 19:11-15.** The image now shifts to the inability of Egypt's leaders and their advisers to understand and remedy their situation.

■ **Isaiah 19:16-25.** The prose additions are arranged in a meaningful sequence. The first addition (vv. 16-17) continues the theme of internal confusion (as in vv. 11-15), but moves further. The Egyptians realize that the Lord is acting against them. Then, cities within Egypt begin to worship the Lord (v. 18). The Egyptians as a whole begin to turn to the true religion (vv. 19-22). Then Assyria joins them in such worship (v. 23). Finally, God's blessing, once given only to Israel, is extended to the other nations (vv. 24-25).

■ **Isaiah 20:1.** The year this verse refers to is likely around 711 BC. States in Palestine have decided to revolt against Assyria. The Palestinian states are assuming that Egypt will come to their aid.

■ **Isaiah 20:2.** "At that time" refers to a summit meeting in Jerusalem around 714 BC, when the possibility of revolt against Assyria was discussed. The prophet had spoken against revolt on that occasion as well (Isaiah 18:1-6).

■ **Isaiah 20:3-4.** For captives of war treated in this fashion, see the note on Isaiah 7:20.

■ **Isaiah 21.** The chapter may be divided into three distinct prophecies, as indicated by the headings in verses 1, 11, and 13. Their common theme seems to be events in the desert.

■ **Isaiah 21:1.** Negev is translated as "southland" here.

■ **Isaiah 21:2.** Presumably, it is God who speaks, authorizing the Elamites to attack Babylon (v. 9). For previous mention of the Medes in this role, see Isaiah 13:17-22. This passage, concerning events around 540 BC, is far removed in time from chapter 20. This verse probably comes from the prophet's disciples.

■ **Isaiah 21:6-9.** It is unclear whether the riders are former captives who were liberated from Babylon by the Elamites, or the Elamites themselves who have swept on through the city.

■ **Isaiah 21:10.** This prophecy is addressed either to Jerusalem (which the Babylonians destroyed in 587 BC), or to the exiles in Babylonia who have been there since that date.

■ **Isaiah 21:11-12.** Dumah seems to be a city in Seir (Edom). That area is in great distress, symbolized by *night*. Messengers from there come to a *watchman* (the prophet?). They inquire, in effect, if there is light at the end of the tunnel. "Not yet," he says, "but check back later." It is not clear what the specific historical situation is, or why such a prophecy would have been preserved.

■ **Isaiah 21:13-15.** We cannot say what has happened to the caravan of Dedanites, or why the inhabitants of the oasis at Tema should help them, or why this event was of interest to the prophet. Perhaps the event is connected with Babylonian oppression of Dedanites, or with flight from the fall of Babylon.

■ **Isaiah 21:16-17.** The tribe of Kedar lived southeast of Palestine, and its territory included Dedan. This prose addition to the previous poetic prophecy switches from sympathy to hostility (see also 16:12-13, where there is a change in mood and literary style as Moab is discussed). What caused the change in mood is not clear.

■ **Isaiah 22.** This chapter is concerned with the premature rejoicing at deliverance from foreign invasion (vv. 1-14). The chapter also discusses the denunciation of a high governmental official (vv. 15-25).

■ **Isaiah 22:1-14.** This section may have been composed in stages. The section most likely to have been written by the prophet himself is verses 1-4 and 12-14. In any case, the sense of the whole can most easily be grasped by reading those verses as a summary.

■ **Isaiah 22:1-2.** The occasion for rejoicing is suggested by verse 2, with its mention of battle. Possibly, the event described is the withdrawal of the Assyrian army in 701 BC.

■ **Isaiah 22:2.** "Your slain" seems to refer, not to those killed in combat, but to those who fled, were taken captive, or who were executed during the siege of 701 BC. Such a situation, suggests the prophet, hardly calls for rejoicing.

■ **Isaiah 22:4.** Why the prophet weeps bitter tears is made clear in verses 12-14.

■ **Isaiah 22:12.** The activity of the Assyrians should have produced a desire for repentance (see comments on Isaiah 1:9, 21-31; 10:22).

■ **Isaiah 22:13.** Instead of repentance, the crisis with Assyria seems to have produced self-confidence and wild abandon. It has made Judah blinder than ever to the people's true status in the eyes of God, just as the prophet's commission anticipated (6:9-10).

■ **Isaiah 22:14.** The prophet's final remark is, in effect, "This is not God's last word on the situation."

■ **Isaiah 22:15.** Shebna's position ("steward / palace administrator") is perhaps comparable to the Secretary of State in the United States government.

■ **Isaiah 22:16.** Hewing a tomb seems to be insufficient grounds for the prophet's anger. Perhaps the official's pride is what caused Isaiah to be so angry at him.

■ **Isaiah 22:20.** Eliakim and Shebna are mentioned as government officials in Isaiah 36:3 and 2 Kings 18:18. Presumably, Eliakim will receive Shebna's office when the latter is taken into exile (v. 18).

■ **Isaiah 22:25.** The prophecy that began in verse 20 ("In that day") expresses great confidence in Eliakim. The one contained in verse 25 (also with the introductory phrase, "In that day") takes a negative attitude toward him. These two verses reflect the opinions of different generations. The prophecies were probably not written by the same person or at the same time.

DIMENSION THREE: WHAT DOES THE BIBLE MEAN TO ME?

Chapters 18–23, which we are now studying, are really a part of chapters 13–23, which we began to study in lesson 3. Therefore, they do not introduce a large number of new theological problems and ideas. This provides us with a pause to revive questions from previous lessons that may have been passed over or inadequately discussed. Here are some of the opportunities.

Isaiah 18:7—A Golden Age

Isaiah 18:7 is similar in tone to the hopes expressed in 2:2-4 and 14:1-2 (see lesson 1 and the discussion of 2:2-4). Such an expectation of a golden age is outlined in 19:19-25, which is remarkable in its inclusiveness. Given the extent of conflict and polarization we are experiencing in most, if not all, of our institutions and societal structures, what would it take to achieve some measure of unity, cooperation, and trust? If Christian churches of different denominations (or even within denominations) cannot agree and be at peace with one another, how might we see God's response to our disharmony? What can individual Christians do to work toward a more golden age?

Isaiah 21:1-10 is concerned with the fate of Babylonia, some one hundred fifty years after the death of Isaiah. Isaiah could not possibly have written those verses himself. His followers surely are responsible for this part of the book. This assertion helps to clarify the fact that the Book of Isaiah has grown over the generations. As the prophet's followers sought to understand the action of God in their own time and in view of Isaiah's original teachings, they added to the text. If the question on authorship and the value of the text was not discussed in lesson 3, now may be a good time to do so.

Authorship may also raise questions of authority. If one portion of Scripture is not exactly what it seems to be, based on exegetical, archeological, and historical discoveries, does that undermine in any way the authority of what the Scripture means? How does the role of interpretation affect how we believe and what we gain from the text?

Isaiah 19:23-25—Historical Accuracy

A prior problem surfaces in a more intense way. In lesson 3, we discussed historical correctness and the value of the text. There, the problem was a minor one; the anticipated destruction of Babylon at the hands of the Medes came instead at the hand of the Persians. Nonetheless, Babylonian oppression of the Judean exiles was brought to an end. The Israelites were allowed to return to their homeland. But now, the problem with fulfillment would seem to be more serious. The writer of Isaiah 19:23-25 anticipates that Egypt, Assyria, and Israel will coexist as worshipers of the Lord. They will be a united source of blessing to others. That anticipation did not come true. It never can. Assyria as a nation, and indeed as a culture, came to an end when it was incorporated into the Babylonian Empire in 612 BC.

Which of the following do you think is a more adequate appraisal of Isaiah 19:23-25? (1) One could scarcely ask for a clearer rejection of biblical literalism or of the verbal inspiration of Scripture. (2) Perhaps, at some time soon after this prophecy was spoken, some Egyptians and some Assyrians did begin to worship Israel's God. This move might have been a brief and limited fulfillment, but it was a fulfillment. (3) Christianity is a much later successor to Israelite religion: the new Israel. Christianity flourished in both Egypt (the Coptic Church) and the area of the former Assyrian Empire (the Nestorian Church). Perhaps Christianity is an indirect fulfillment of the prophecy. (4) Perhaps Egypt and Assyria are not literally used, but are symbols for enemies of the people of God. They are always with us. What we want to understand is the writer's *spirit* (intention) and not his *letter* (literal expression). Thus, what is expressed here is an inspiring expectation. It is a hope we should continually strive for, and one toward which the love for God drives us.

In addition to choosing what historical lens or supposition we may follow, another approach may be used. Rather than relying exclusively on the accuracy of the text as history, suppose the Scripture is considered for the theological point it is making. What difference does this make in considering the prophecies that God will make things right?

See, the LORD is going to lay waste the earth / and devastate it; / he will ruin its face / and scatter its inhabitants. (24:1)

THE ISAIAH APOCALYPSE

Isaiah 24–27

DIMENSION ONE: WHAT DOES THE BIBLE SAY?

Answer these questions by reading Isaiah 24

1. Unlike previous prophecies that have been addressed either to Judah or to foreign nations, this one has a much wider problem in view. Against whom does God now take action? (24:1, 4, 17)

2. What causes God to take action against the earth? (24:5)

3. While the majority of the world's people may be dejected at the prospect of divine judgment, what reaction does a minority of the people have? (24: 14)

4. What is the final outcome of God's judgment? (24:23)

Answer these questions by reading Isaiah 25

5. For what does the poet now thank God? (25:2)

6. What will the nations now do? (25:3)

7. Where will the center of God's rule be, after the judgment of the nations? (25:6, 7, 10)

Answer these questions by reading Isaiah 26

8. What is to be the people's attitude? (26:4)

9. What does the poet want to happen? (26:5)

10. How long are Judah's present difficulties expected to last? (26:20)

Answer these questions by reading Isaiah 27

11. What standard introductory phrases mark the beginning of individual prophecies? (27:1, 2, 6, 12)

12. What symbol does Isaiah use for evil and chaos? (27:1)

13. What is God's future care of the community compared to? (27:2-3)

14. What actions are prescribed in order to remove Jacob's sin? (27:9)

15. What will happen to the exiles? (27:13)

DIMENSION TWO: WHAT DOES THE BIBLE MEAN?

■ **Background.** Chapters 24–27 are another distinct collection within the larger Book of Isaiah. They are a third stage of reflection on the problems God faces in dealing with human beings. Chapters 1–12 were concerned with the internal affairs of Judah. Those prophecies were introduced either as a vision (1:1) or as a word (2:1). Chapters 13–23 dealt with Judah in relationship to neighbors who had become hostile oppressors. Those chapters were introduced as prophecies (13:1).

Chapters 24–27 contain a series of poetic images of God's judgment on the entire earth. Judgment will lead to the ultimate redemption of Israel. No longer do we read of specific tyrants or oppressive empires. The world has been cursed because of the sins of its inhabitants (24:4-6). Everything will be cleansed, heaven above and earth beneath (24:21-23). Israel will become a "fruitful vineyard" of "the LORD" (27:2-3).

The sequence of these three sections is logical. The judgment that chapters 1–12 anticipated has become a reality in chapters 13-23. However, the solution has now become a problem. The agents of judgment (Assyria and Babylonia) have become prideful obstacles to the will of God. This is only part of a more pervasive problem that is discovered in chapters 24–27. Thus, the concern of God is expanded from local Judean rebellion against the covenant (chaps. 1–12), to the pride of the conqueror (chaps. 13–23), to a creation on the verge of reverting to chaos (chaps. 24–27).

This three-stage development corresponds to three generations of theological thought. The first stage is primarily by the prophet himself during the period 743–701 BC (chaps. 1–12). Next Isaiah's followers reuse and add to Isaiah's speeches. This was done during the period of Assyrian and Babylonian domination of Palestine, 733–539 BC (chaps. 13–23). The third stage of reflection on the problems of the world is by an even later generation of the prophet's followers. These reflections come from the postexilic age (after 539 BC), when things did not turn out as well as expected (chaps. 24–27).

The belief that God's problem is far wider than an errant chosen community in Palestine, that it is a world in the grip of sin, leads us toward a theological system of thought called *apocalypticism*. This system begins to develop during the exilic period (587–539 BC). It reaches maturity in the Book of Daniel (second century BC) and in the New Testament.

Chapters 24–27 of Isaiah, which begin to move toward apocalypticism, are sometimes called the Isaiah Apocalypse. This collection of prophecies ends abruptly at chapter 28, where we again hear criticism of an errant Judah by Isaiah, similar to the criticism of chapters 1–12.

■ **Isaiah 24.** The chapter is divided in to four sections. The first section is God's judgment on the entire earth (vv. 1-13). Next comes a song of praise by those who will be vindicated by God's action (vv. 14-16). The third section returns to the judgment theme of verses 1-13. This section stresses the idea that none shall escape judgment (vv. 17-20). The last section deals with a golden age after the judgment (vv. 21-23).

■ **Isaiah 24:1-3.** God's activity in history is often described by prophets with poetic license (see, for example, Habakkuk 3:6, 11). The central concern is that God will right the wrongs of the world. The prophet is not literally describing a catastrophe that might remind one of a nuclear attack.

■ **Isaiah 24:5.** The "everlasting covenant" may be the one enacted at the time of Noah, the ancestor of the entire human race (Genesis 9). This covenant forbade the shedding of innocent blood. Violation of that prohibition contaminates the land itself, as in Numbers 35:33-34, placing it under a curse. A similar thought was advanced earlier by Hosea (4:13).

■ **Isaiah 24:14.** In an abrupt transition, we switch to the reaction of the people of God. They rejoice at judgment on the present world order.

■ **Isaiah 24:21.** In ancient Israelite thought, each nation of the earth was assigned to the care of what we would now call a "guardian angel." The NIV translates the Hebrew word used here as "powers in the heavens above." Within that framework of thought, if God subdues the kings of the earth, their semi-divine guardians are likewise punished. This idea later developed into that of rebellious angels, cast out of heaven and bound with the devil for a time (Revelation 20:1-3). That goes beyond the intent of the present passage, however. This verse seems to suggest that worship of the stars ("powers in the heavens above") will cease, along with oppressive foreign rulers.

■ **Isaiah 25.** This chapter may be divided into two sections. The first section (vv. 1-5) is a poetic song of thanksgiving that an oppressive empire has come to an end. The second section is a vision of an ideal future, which seems to be in two parts, with a new beginning at verse 9.

■ **Isaiah 25:2.** The identification of this capital city remains obscure.

■ **Isaiah 25:3.** Because of what has happened, nations will begin to revere the true Lord who has acted in this fashion.

■ **Isaiah 25:4.** The poor and needy are likely the remnants of Judah.

■ **Isaiah 25:6-12.** Two prophetic expectations seem to have been combined here. Verses 6-8 and 9-12 have differing viewpoints. Note the new beginning at verse 9 and the shift in attitude toward surrounding nations that begins at that point. Aligned with the openness of verses 6-8 are 2:2-4; 11:10; 18:7; 19:19-25. Aligned with the exclusivism and hostility of verses 9-12 are 11:12-16; 14:1-2. (For an earlier expression of hostility toward Moab in particular, see Isaiah 16).

■ **Isaiah 25:7.** A *shroud* is a sign of mourning, and must have been common in the world of conflict that the passage describes. The prophet anticipates that sorrow will come to an end. In the next verse, he tells why that will be so.

■ **Isaiah 25:8.** The prophet's concern is not universal mortality (that is, how sad it is that we must die). Rather, he speaks about the "people's disgrace," the oppressed Judeans. The death spoken of is slaughter, which will soon cease. Later, the apocalypticists will develop this expectation into the concept of the resurrection of the dead.

■ **Isaiah 26.** This chapter is one of the more difficult chapters of the book. When it was composed is not certain. Scholars disagree about whether it is a single speech or several speeches strung together. Also, translation of the chapter is difficult at many points. Perhaps the following division will help clarify the chapter's meaning.

The first section is a song to be sung at the time of Judah's deliverance from a world power (vv. 1-6). Section two is a prayer of confidence in God (vv. 7-15); it consists of a confession of trust (vv. 7-9), a proverb (v. 10), a petition for deliverance (v. 11), and an assurance of being heard (vv. 12-15). The next section is a lament about present realities (vv. 16-19). Finally, there is an instruction to the community (vv. 20-21).

> Isaiah 26:1. The "strong city" is Jerusalem, now secure.
> Isaiah 26:2. Pilgrims now come to the holy city, to praise God for what has happened.
> Isaiah 26:5. The "lofty city" is apparently the former oppressor referred to in 25:2; 24:10.

Isaiah 26:18. The inability of the community to escape its present oppressors is compared with a woman in false labor. She has much pain but no results.

■ **Isaiah 26:18-19.** This section is filled with translation problems, as a comparison of English translations shows. (compare the NRSV, NIV, and CEV). No one is positive how to translate this passage, but the overall meaning of the chapter is clear. The Judean community will be delivered from oppression. The "dead" seem to be the entire community, rather than individuals. They rise and awake in national restoration.

■ **Isaiah 27.** This chapter is a collection of miscellaneous portraits of the future, ideal age. They begin with the formal introduction "In that day. . . ."

■ **Isaiah 27:1.** Several ancient Near Eastern creation stories envisioned "the beginning" as the time when the chief god brought order out of a pre-existing chaos. Most often, the chaos is described as a raging sea. The chaos is personified as a dragon (sometimes named Leviathan, Rahab, or Tiamat). The chaos/monster, although subdued, was used by apocalyptic theologians to explain present difficulties. God's righteous dominion over nature and humans was not yet total. Thus, before a golden age could arrive, Leviathan must be slain. This Leviathan was not yet identified with the devil or with the serpent in the garden of Eden.

■ **Isaiah 27:2-5.** This passage is the opposite of 5:1-7. Perhaps 27:2-5 was written with that earlier passage in mind. Whereas God formerly allowed the "vineyard" (Judah, and especially Jerusalem) to be destroyed, God now will nourish and protect it.

■ **Isaiah 27:4.** God's wrath against Judah has now vanished. The thorns and briars that formerly threatened the vineyard (5:6) will be destroyed.

■ **Isaiah 27:7-11.** Little can be said with confidence about this difficult passage. Who are "he," "her," and "those"? And who are those "who struck her"? Is this passage about events in the past or a future time? And where is the "fortified city" (v. 10)? Taking a cue from the present context (v. 5), the meaning might be that God has indeed smitten the Northern Kingdom (Israel/Jacob). But God has dealt with them less severely than with their oppressors, and with the capital city of 24:10; 25:2; 26:5. In any case, what has happened to Jacob will serve a positive end of forgiveness and renewal. But exactly what events the passage refers to remain obscure to us. The fortified city, now abandoned, is the previously mentioned capital city of the oppressing nation.

■ **Isaiah 27:12-13.** In the ideal future age, all the scattered exiles, from both north and south, will return and worship God on the holy mountain (Zion). This is a fitting conclusion to the so-called Isaiah Apocalypse (chaps. 24–27), and is a theme found elsewhere (14:1-2; 11:11; 10:20-23).

DIMENSION THREE: WHAT DOES THE BIBLE MEAN TO ME?

We have seen many different types of reflection in the Book of Isaiah. We have read reflections by the prophet on life in eighth-century Judah (chaps. 1–12). We have read reflections by the prophet's early disciples on foreign domination during the seventh and early sixth centuries (chaps. 13–23). Isaiah's more remote followers reflected on the continual travails of the postexilic age (chaps. 24–27).

How the various writers' perceptions of the problem have shifted has been interesting. The shift has been from faithless Judah to God's foreign agents of discipline—who then become proud and oppressive, to an entire world in need of transformation. Correspondingly, the proposed remedy has shifted from repentance, to defeat of a specific oppressor, to liberation from all oppression by means of a catastrophic event that will usher in an ideal age of divine rule. The shift is from exhortation for the recovery of Israel's ancient ideals, to despair for the future. What is needed is an act that will swallow up death (25:8) and end the power of chaos (27: 1).

What is God's main problem and solution in the present? Is God's problem in the present a faithless church that tolerates and conforms to the values of the world? How can we put the Bible's ideals into practice, as the prophet Isaiah had in mind?

What evidence indicates that the world is in the grip of the power of sin? How can the church, by repentance and action, change that reality? Can only God do so, through radical intervention and transformation? If so, what is the role of the Church and of people of faith?

Is one perspective (Isaiah's or his followers') more accurate (or authoritative) than the other? How can the two perspectives stand side by side within the Scripture?

People of Zion, who live in Jerusalem, you will weep no more.
(30:19)

JUDAH, PRESENT AND FUTURE
Isaiah 28–35

DIMENSION ONE: WHAT DOES THE BIBLE SAY?

Answer these questions by reading Isaiah 28

1. To what audience is this word addressed? (28:1, 3, 14)

2. What is Isaiah now condemning? (28:1, 3, 7, 15)

3. Who has the Lord chosen to educate Judah? (28:11)

4. What was the attitude of the Judeans toward the possibility of catastrophe in their international relations? (28:15)

5. What is Isaiah comparing himself to? (28:24-28)

Answer these questions by reading Isaiah 29

6. By what name does the prophet call Jerusalem? (29:1, 2)

7. Why are the people unable to perceive their fate? (29:9-10)

8. To what does Isaiah compare those who try to hide from God? (29:15-16)

Answer these questions by reading Isaiah 30

9. What political policy does the prophet condemn? (30:2)

10. How does the prophet ensure survival of his message? (30:8)

11. On what are the people tempted to rely? (30:16)

12. What will the future ideal age be like? (30:20-21)

Answer this question by reading Isaiah 31

13. What will happen to the Egyptians and their allies? (31:3)

Answer this question by reading Isaiah 32

14. What will the leaders in the ideal age be like? (32:1)

Answer these questions by reading Isaiah 33

15. What will happen to Judah's destroyers? (33:1)

16. What must one do to be worthy of the new age? (33:15-16)

Answer these questions by reading Isaiah 34

17. What audience is now addressed? (34:1, 2)

18. What nation is the object of God's wrath? (34:5, 6, 9)

19. To what source does the speaker turn for confirmation of his words? (34:16)

Answer this question by reading Isaiah 35

20. On whom does a new future depend? (35:4)

DIMENSION TWO: WHAT DOES THE BIBLE MEAN?

■ **Background.** Chapters 28–35 contain various kinds of poems and address a wide range of historical situations. They may have been composed over several centuries. Much of chapters 28–32 concern Judah's present and are related in theme to chapters 1–12. The prophet himself probably composed much of these chapters. Most of chapters 33–35 concern Judah's future and are related in theme to chapters 13–23 and 24–27. The prophet's disciples, over several generations, are likely the authors.

■ **Isaiah 28:1.** The "wreath" and "fading flower," described as "the head of a fertile valley," possibly refer to Samaria, the political and religious center. Whether the term *drunkards* is used in the literal sense, or as a metaphor for blindness to the political fate of the nation, is uncertain.

■ **Isaiah 28:2.** The one ordained by God to destroy Ephraim is stated elsewhere to be Assyria.

■ **Isaiah 28:7-22.** All of this passage is directed against the South. That the intended audience is Judah is clear from verses 14 and 16.

■ **Isaiah 28:9.** "He" may be God, as is suggested in verses 11-13. Or "he" could be the prophet.

■ **Isaiah 28:10.** The people object that they are being treated like children. A child must be taught the rudiments of religion letter by letter. The prophet implies that the people will reject this attempt to teach them something they already know well.

■ **Isaiah 28:11.** Judah has rejected instruction by the prophet. God will now use the Assyrians, who speak with an alien tongue.

■ **Isaiah 28:15.** The "overwhelming scourge" would be the Assyrian invasion of Palestine.

■ **Isaiah 28:16.** Even as destruction is taking place, God is rebuilding. If the people can, by listening to the prophet, understand what God is doing amidst the current catastrophe, then the community will be renewed. It will be constructed with such building blocks as "justice" and "righteousness" (v. 17).

■ **Isaiah 28:19.** The message is that the community deserves its impending fate; it is the will of God.

■ **Isaiah 28:21.** Mount Perazim was the site of a defeat of the Philistines (2 Samuel 5:17-21). Gibeon was the site of a defeat of the Canaanites (Joshua 10:7-10).

■ **Isaiah 28:23-29.** This section is more like wisdom literature than prophetic writing. These verses do not condemn the present or anticipate a better future. They stress that action should be taken at the appropriate season.

■ **Isaiah 29.** This chapter deals with the siege of Jerusalem (vv. 1-8), a lack of perception on the part of the people (vv. 9-16), and a better future (vv. 17-24).

■ **Isaiah 29:1-8.** This passage may be a single composition or two prophecies that have been combined. Verses 1-4 are possibly by Isaiah, with the others being additions.

■ **Isaiah 29:1.** *Ariel* is a difficult word. It probably is an ancient name for Jerusalem, meaning something like altar (for burnt sacrifice). The expression "where David settled" calls to mind God's promises to that place (Psalm 132:13-18). The phrase also points to the contrast between present wickedness and that golden age. The concluding part of the verse seems to condemn mindless ritual at a time of great crisis.

■ **Isaiah 29:2.** The ancient altar will be consumed by its own fire ("like an Ariel").

■ **Isaiah 29:5.** The word *but* is misleading, since it implies that the attackers would not succeed. This interpretation is in keeping with chapters 36–39 (where the attacking Assyrians are said to have withdrawn from Jerusalem). However, the Hebrew text merely has *and*, which would allow the threat to continue.

■ **Isaiah 29:6.** If the Lord's visitation is for the punishment of the Judeans themselves, then it is only at verse 7 that a positive word begins.

■ **Isaiah 29:9-12.** Verses 9-10 may be a genuine word of Isaiah to which a later prose section has been added. The people cannot perceive their danger during the Assyrian crisis, because God has blinded them to it.

■ **Isaiah 29:14.** "Wonder upon wonder" is not a well-chosen phrase for this threatening context, since we ordinarily use it in a positive way. Compare other translations.

■ **Isaiah 29:17-24.** These verses show a sudden transition from past to future. This transition suggests a different situation and perhaps a different speaker from the previous verses. This passage is likely by the disciples, rather than Isaiah.

■ **Isaiah 29:18.** Does the speaker refer to the by-now written words of Isaiah, which future generations will finally appreciate?

■ **Isaiah 30.** This chapter contains three prophecies stating that no security may be found in alliance with Egypt (vv. 1-5, 6-7, 15-17). Possibly the prophecies are concerned with the crisis in 701 BC, and are by Isaiah. Verses 8-14 contain a prophecy, probably by Isaiah, that announces judgment on rebellious Judah. Verses 18-26 describe a better future for Jerusalem. Verses 27-28 give two views of the destruction of the oppressive Assyrians.

■ **Isaiah 30:2.** The person who is not consulted refers to the prophet as a resource for knowledge of the divine will.

■ **Isaiah 30:4.** Zoan and Hanes are northern Egyptian cities under the control of the Ethiopian (Cushite) dynasty (see notes to 18:1-2). That this dynasty's control is that far north does not guarantee help for Judah, suggests Isaiah.

■ **Isaiah 30:6.** The harsh and sparsely populated desert (the Negev) was sometimes thought to be inhabited by fantastic beasts, real and imaginary. By "the envoys" the prophet apparently refers to Judean ambassadors. Laden with gifts, they were on their way to seek Egyptian aid.

■ **Isaiah 30:7.** The powers of Rahab, subdued by God at creation, cannot again reemerge. Similarly, Egypt is powerless. Her reputation far exceeds reality. This *Rahab* is a legendary monster of chaos, not the brave woman who helped the spies in Joshua's time (Joshua 2).

■ **Isaiah 30:8-14.** For a similar command to write down prophecy for future use, see 8:1-4, 16. We do not know for sure what "it" (v. 8) refers to. It could be the previous prophecy (provided that verses 6-7 and 8-14 are part of a continuous speech), or the entire collection by Isaiah that we are now studying (chaps. 28–31).

■ **Isaiah 30:12.** "This message" is verses 9-11.

■ **Isaiah 30:15.** The prophet now sums up his message to the present generation amidst the Assyrian crisis. He preaches repentance, rest, quietness, and trust.

■ **Isaiah 30:17.** A thousand Judeans will flee from one enemy. Those who survive will be so few that they will be as conspicuous as a flagpole atop a hill.

■ **Isaiah 30:19.** The theme of this verse may be compared with 25:8 and 35:10. The theme suggests a late origin for the prophecies.

■ **Isaiah 30:20.** God's future actions in history, even when adverse, will be readily understandable, in contrast to the long and perplexing calamities of the recent past. "Teachers" could refer to God or to human leaders who are hidden now.

■ **Isaiah 30:25.** The "towers" are the fortifications of the oppressor- nation, which will soon be destroyed.

■ **Isaiah 30:28.** The phrase "up to the neck" echoes Isaiah 8:8, and may be meant as a reversal of 8:8. Just as Judah was once threatened, now its tormentors will be.

■ **Isaiah 30:32.** Since the enemy is compared with an animal about to be sacrificed (v. 33), the musical instruments may refer to music played in the Temple when sacrifices are made.

■ **Isaiah 30:33.** "Topheth" (the burning place) is an abandoned, pagan site of human sacrifice outside Jerusalem. The reference to the king may be a pun.

■ **Isaiah 31.** It is difficult to divide this chapter into its original speech forms, or decide how many speeches there were. One section seems to be verses 1-3, a typical woe prophecy (as in 28:1-4; 29:15-16; 30:1-5). Then we find two sections of poetry separated by a prose section of entirely different concern.

■ **Isaiah 31:1-3.** The theme here is the same as 30:1-5, 6-7, and 15-17. The people of Judah trust alliance with Egypt more than they trust God. This will result in their destruction. We may, therefore, conclude that this is a genuine prophecy from Isaiah during the time of the crisis in 701 BC.

■ **Isaiah 31:2.** The prophet has anticipated God's action in the present, and the divine plan has not changed.

■ **Isaiah 31:6-7.** This theme is common among the prophet's prose-writing disciples.

■ **Isaiah 31:8.** What the speaker has in mind by "not of mortals" is unclear. The remainder of the verse, "will be put to forced labor," which assumes a human power as God's agent, shows he is not clear on this phrase himself.

■ **Isaiah 31:9.** The identity of the "stronghold" (or "rock") is also unclear.

■ **Isaiah 32.** The chapter may be divided into the following themes: (1) an ideal age of righteousness (vv. 1-8), (2) judgment by means of agricultural failure and national defeat (vv. 9-14), and (3) a future age of security (vv. 15-20). The last two themes probably form a single composition.

■ **Isaiah 32:4-8.** This condition is the reverse of past and present reality as described in Isaiah 5:18-23.

■ **Isaiah 32:9-14.** The women are not accused of pride or immorality (cf. 3:16-26). Since they lead the rejoicing at the time of harvest, they will wail at the time of agricultural failure.

■ **Isaiah 32:19.** This verse is puzzling, if "the city" refers to Jerusalem. Jerusalem has just been promised God's Spirit and blessing (vv. 15-18). This verse could have been misplaced in later copying and may belong with verse 14, prior to the time of God's blessing. However, the city may not be Jerusalem, but the capital of the oppressive world empire. Then this verse would be a later addition.

■ **Isaiah 33–35.** The collection of woe prophecies (chaps. 28–32), by Isaiah himself, seems now to have ended. Increasingly now, the prophecies will be by the prophet's followers.

■ **Isaiah 33.** Verse 1 is a denunciation of the "destroyer." Verses 2-6 are a prayer of petition for relief, followed by expectation of deliverance. Verses 7-9 further describe the present. Verses 10-13 are the Lord's answer, as anticipated by the speaker. Verses 14-16 describe those who will be worthy to worship in a renewed Jerusalem. Verses 17-22 describe the new age. Verse 23 returns to the theme of military spoils, resuming verse 4. Verse 24 deals with health in the new age.

■ **Isaiah 33:1.** The destroyer is not named, possibly to protect the speaker and his community from reprisal. The prophet's disciples in the postexilic age usually speak vaguely of "the city" (see note to 32:19). Note also the previous use of *Babylon* and *Assyria* to refer to whatever oppressive powers is in control at the moment.

■ **Isaiah 33:4.** Apparently, such spoils will not be available to Judah.

■ **Isaiah 33:7-9.** A specific historical incident is probably being described, rather than life in general.

■ **Isaiah 33:11-12.** The "you" is the enemy, now directly addressed. The "peoples" presumably are the nationalities of the soldiers that accompany the enemy.

■ **Isaiah 33:14.** God's judgment extends beyond the enemy to the wicked within Judah. The wicked fear that they will be slain in the attack, which will be God's judgment upon them.

■ **Isaiah 33:17.** To "see the king" apparently means to understand and obey God. That God is meant, rather than the human ruler, is suggested is verse 22. A "land that stretches afar" would mean wide dominion and security from neighbors.

■ **Isaiah 33:21.** Security from ships may suggest that the enemy was from the Aegean Sea and descended from Alexander the Great. If so, then this vision would be dated to the late fourth century BC at the earliest.

■ **Isaiah 33:23.** "Your" refers to the enemy, whose ships do not save them in the impending judgment.

■ **Isaiah 34.** This chapter has two distinct phases. Verses 1-4 deal with impending judgment on the earth; verses 5-17 are a judgment on Edom.

■ **Isaiah 34:4.** The speaker here uses traditional, liturgical, poetic, and exaggerated language. Heaven and earth continue to exist. All this imagery is a mere prelude to Judean exiles being allowed to return to Jerusalem (chap. 35).

■ **Isaiah 34:5-17.** Hostility toward Edom is rare in Isaiah. Since this attitude arose mainly in the exilic and postexilic age, it seems safe to conclude that this passage is from the prophet's late followers.

■ **Isaiah 34:6.** Bozrah is a strong fortress in Edom.

■ **Isaiah 34:8.** "Zion's cause" results from the fact that the Edomites have constantly taken advantage of Judah's weakness, beginning with the Exile in 586 BC.

■ **Isaiah 34:16.** The reference to "the scroll of the LORD" is a graphic way of saying that God has destined these creatures to inhabit Edom's territory. It is written in the book of fate, or as we would say, "It's in the cards."

■ **Isaiah 35.** This collection (chaps. 28–35) ends on a positive note: the return of God's people to Zion.

■ **Isaiah 35:1.** The scattered Judeans must return home through the desert, by means of a highway (v. 8). A contrast with the barrenness that has been promised Edom seems to be intended.

■ **Isaiah 35:2.** "They" are probably the fainthearted Jews, as in verse 4.

■ **Isaiah 35:3.** It is not clear who is being exhorted to strengthen the weak. God addresses either the prophet or members of God's heavenly council (angelic beings).

■ **Isaiah 35:5-6.** It is not clear whether the speaker refers to physical, miraculous cures, or to spiritual recovery. The continuation of the verse supports the idea that a spiritual recovery is intended. This recovery will happen because of a return to Zion.

■ **Isaiah 35:8.** The image of the "highway" back home was used at the conclusion of chapters 1–10 (see also 11:16).

DIMENSION THREE: WHAT DOES THE BIBLE MEAN TO ME?

Isaiah 28:9-22—God's Strange Instrument

The audience apparently believes that it is being insulted by the prophet. He treats them as if they are children who must be lectured on the rudiments of the faith, letter by letter. God responds that this approach has failed to bring about change. Another approach, strange and alien, must now be tried. The teachers will be the Assyrians.

To the audience, this new message is doubly insulting. Not only are they in serious need of correction; they will be corrected by those seemingly least qualified to do it! The Assyrians did not follow God's ethical guidelines. They did not even acknowledge that they were in Palestine at God's bidding! To the average Judean, they were pagans. Where else in the Bible have outsiders become God's instruments?

Where else in the Bible were speakers from within disdained by the majority, even though they spoke the truth? What insight and guidance do these instances provide for churches in the present? Can you think of instances, within your lifetime, when prophets were rebuffed who should have been heeded? When have secular persons protested injustice, while religious institutions were silent?

Can we move to our national life and make similar observations? When has God's hand been at work in judgment on our society through the activity of our enemies?

Reflect for a few minutes on your past and present relationships with persons. When has the truth about you been spoken by someone who dislikes you? Can God's judgment be expressed through those whose own concern is malice for others? Or, are such thoughts insane, as the prophet's audience said? Would we, had we been there, have sided with the prophet or his audience? Why?

The time will surely come when everything in your palace, and all that your predecessors have stored up until this day, will be carried off to Babylon. (39:6)

7

ISAIAH AND HEZEKIAH

Isaiah 36–39

DIMENSION ONE: WHAT DOES THE BIBLE SAY?

Answer these questions by reading Isaiah 36

1. In what way does this chapter begin differently from all of the previous ones? (36:1)

2. Why has the king of Assyria sent his army against Judah? (36:5)

3: What foreign power have the Judeans expected to come to their aid? (36:6)

4. What deity has summoned the Assyrian army into Judah, according to the Assyrian general? (36:10)

5. Why has the Lord summoned the Assyrians? (36:7)

Answer these questions by reading Isaiah 37

6. What does Hezekiah hope for? (37:4)

7. How have the Assyrian plans offended the Lord? (37:29)

8. What does the prophet expect? (37:35)

Answer these questions by reading Isaiah 38

9. What is the basis of Hezekiah's appeal for a longer life? (38:3)

10. What is the cause of the king's illness? (38:17)

11. What can't the dead do? (38:18-19)

Answer these questions by reading Isaiah 39

12. What enemy nation now emerges? (39:1)

13. What was Hezekiah's attitude toward this potential ally against Assyria? (39:2)

14. What future does the prophet expect at the hands of the Babylonians? (39:6-7)

DIMENSION TWO: WHAT DOES THE BIBLE MEAN?

■ **Background.** Chapters 36–39 of Isaiah are largely prose, whereas what comes before and after them is almost entirely poetry. When such change occurs, the modern interpreter should be aware of the possibility of a new audience, a new historical situation, and possibly a new speaker.

In terms of theme, chapters 36–38 stress that Jerusalem is secure from conquest by the Assyrians. You should remember that such confidence conflicts with Isaiah's expectation that this enemy would indeed destroy the city (Isaiah 5:1-7; 6:11-13; 7:18-25; 30:12-14). However, other passages in the book express confidence in the city's security, such as 16:4-7; 30:29-33; 31:8-9. Since those optimistic passages seem to reflect the opinion of the prophet's disciples, we may wonder whether chapters 36–38 are not from a later period as well. This idea would help to account for the fact that Isaiah does not speak in the first person. His actions and words are described in the third person: "Isaiah . . . sent" (37:21), "Isaiah . . . went" (38:1), and "Isaiah said" (39:5).

With the aid of notes in your Bible, you will discover that Isaiah 36–39 is parallel to 2 Kings 18:13–20:19. In fact, the wording is identical from 2 Kings 18:19 onward. Why this repetition? Was one passage copied from the other? If so, in which book did the passage originate? Read both sections in their contexts. You will note that the account in Second Kings is an essential part of the storyline. Deleting the passage in Second Kings leaves a noticeable gap. By contrast, the account may be dropped from Isaiah without leaving a trace. So the passage probably has been borrowed from Second Kings, perhaps by the prophet's disciples. The purpose would have been to give a more complete report of Isaiah's ministry; all the stories of Isaiah in a single collection. Why locate them here after chapter 35; perhaps because the previous collection of prophecies, chapters 28–35, stress the security of Jerusalem. These stories will provide a continuity of theme.

The event that the passage describes is one already familiar to readers of the Book of Isaiah: the Assyrian invasion of 701 BC (see the note to Isaiah 22:1-2). King Hezekiah of Judah has decided not to honor his alliance with Assyria. The Assyrians have arrived to force his compliance (see the notes to Isaiah 20:1-2; 31:1-3). Later, the Assyrians withdraw. This move seems to have caught the prophet by surprise (Isaiah 22). But he interprets the withdrawal as a sign of God's graciousness (Isaiah 1:9).

The portrait just sketched, from genuine Isaiah prophecies, differs at points from the account in chapters 36–37.

■ **Isaiah 36–37.** These two chapters are meant to be read as a continuous story. However, as you read it, you may notice that more than one account has been combined. Look for repetitions and differing points of view.

■ **Isaiah 36:1.** No other chapter in Isaiah begins by dating the year of the king's reign. By contrast, narratives often begin this way in the books of Kings (see, for example, 1 Kings 15:1; 2 Kings 3:1; 12:1; 13:1). This introduction suggests that the story has been borrowed from Kings.

■ **Isaiah 36:2.** The word *Rabshaketh* in the NRSV refers to an office rather than a name. In the NIV, it is translated as "field commander."

■ **Isaiah 36:6.** For previous mention of Judah's reliance on Egypt as an ally against Assyria, see Isaiah 20:5-6; 30:2; 31:1-3.

■ **Isaiah 36:7.** Hezekiah, in an effort to reform Judean worship, had closed many traditional sanctuaries. He has encouraged the people to come to Jerusalem instead, "this altar" (see 2 Kings 18:1-6). This effort probably provoked opposition from local priests; some of them may have thought that the king should be punished (just as the Assyrian general proposes).

■ **Isaiah 36:10.** The Assyrian general proposes that he is the Lord's agent. He has been sent to punish Judah. Judah has not only destroyed traditional sanctuaries (v. 7), but has broken its alliance with Assyria. Such alliances involved the taking of oaths in God's name. When oaths are broken, one has angered the deity by swearing falsely.

■ **Isaiah 36:11.** Aramaic was the language of international diplomacy at the time.

■ **Isaiah 37:3.** The country's dangerous situation is illustrated by an analogy. The situation is like a woman who develops complications during childbirth and is in extreme danger.

■ **Isaiah 37:22-32.** The *you* of verses 22-39 is the king of Assyria. The *you* of verse 30 is Hezekiah. The *I* of verses 24-25 is the king of Assyria. The *I* of verse 26 is the Lord.

■ **Isaiah 37:26.** The king of Assyria should not boast about his conquests, as if they resulted from his own initiative and ability. In fact, the Lord is using him in accordance with previous divine plans.

■ **Isaiah 38.** Although the chapter has a single theme (Hezekiah's sickness), it has the following parts, possibly of separate origin: (1) a prose account of the king's affliction and of God's promise (vv. 1-8); (2) a poetic prayer of thanksgiving, perhaps a traditional prayer that is now placed in the mouth of the king (vv. 10-20); and (3) details of the story that apparently were accidentally left out (vv. 21-22).

■ **Isaiah 38:8.** Use of the word *dial* in the NRSV is an interpretation of the translator. The NIV translates the word more literally as *stairway*.

■ **Isaiah 38:12-13.** The words *you* and *he* refer to God, presumed to be the ultimate source of the king's suffering.

■ **Isaiah 38:16.** This verse is unclear in the context. At such points, compare translations, and if possible, consult a good commentary. The CEV translates the line, "Your words and your deeds bring life to everyone, / including me. / Please make me healthy and strong again."

■ **Isaiah 38:20.** This verse is out of place; it looks forward to the healing that verses 17-19 have already announced as accomplished.

■ **Isaiah 38:21-22.** These verses, in prose, belong back in the prose narrative (vv. 1-8). They seem to be an afterthought, necessary to explain the prose account. How did God heal the king (v. 6)? What prompted the prophet to offer the king a sign (v. 7)? In actuality, these verses are not afterthoughts, but verses that have been accidentally lost from the prose narrative. This fact can be verified by reading the parallel account at 2 Kings 20:7-8.

■ **Isaiah 39:1.** The Babylonian ruler, himself in rebellion against the Assyrians, is seeking an ally in the king of Judah. His gift, therefore, is politically motivated.

■ **Isaiah 39:5-7.** The passage attempts to explain why the Babylonians destroyed the holy city. Earlier, Hezekiah had shown them the wealth of the city and the Temple. Presumably, this destruction was a violation of the sanctity of the place (an offense to God). It may have incited greed that was not soon to be forgotten.

DIMENSION THREE: WHAT DOES THE BIBLE MEAN TO ME?

Isaiah 36–39—Historical Correctness and Faith

Chapters 36–39 of Isaiah present new illustrations of a problem that have arisen previously. Is the text historically correct in its details? For example, could the Assyrians have withdrawn from Jerusalem because Hezekiah promised to pay the tribute they had come to collect? Their own account suggests that this was the case. And, some support may be found in 2 Kings 18:13-16, deleted from the version in Isaiah. Would the Assyrian king withdraw and relinquish what was due, merely because of a rumor (Isaiah 37:7)? How can we explain such a monumental loss as 185,000 soldiers within a single night?

The problem now is compounded because of conflicting accounts of what happened. For example, did the Assyrians withdraw before siege work could even begin (Isaiah 37:33-35)? Or did they, in fact, besiege the city strenuously and for some time? (Isaiah 1:9; 29:1-3).

How important is it to you that various accounts of an event are in total agreement? Is agreement among biblical accounts a matter of faith to you? Do you think these considerations were important to those who told the biblical stories or to those who heard them? Or did they have a different concern? If so, what was their concern? How does (or can) this account inform our faith if we treat it as a record of God's activities and intentions toward us rather than focusing on its historical accuracy in all details?

Isaiah 37—Reinterpretation Within Scripture

When the story of Jerusalem's survival from Assyrian conquest was written, several emphases of the prophet Isaiah were preserved. He had urged the monarch and the citizens of the place to believe in the possibility of deliverance (7:7-9). He had asked them to trust in God rather than in foreign alliances (30:15). He had condemned the arrogance of the Assyrians whom God had summoned to punish the unfaithful Judeans (10:5-19). In these cases, the great prophet would have been pleased that his emphases remained alive in the thought of succeeding generations. But he might have been a bit surprised that new conclusions were reached by those who came after him, and that some of those conclusions were now being proposed as his own.

The punishment of the Assyrians, which Isaiah had expected to happen after they conquered Jerusalem (10:5-19), is now proposed as his expectation on them even before they could approach Jerusalem (37:33-35). The faith that he had proclaimed as a precondition of deliverance (7:9) is now replaced by an assurance of deliverance with no preconditions (37:5-7). Israel is delivered for the sake of David (37:35). In any case, this writing suggests that faithlessness and a failure to trust God are corrected by some kind of punishment. What do you think about the effectiveness of sanctions or punishments in gaining better results? What other methods may work as well? In what ways does genuine transformation take place?

Isaiah 36–37—Is Jerusalem Secure?

Those who composed the story of Jerusalem's deliverance, as we now have it in chapters 36–37, wanted to move the hearer beyond concerns for military tactics and the economy to matters of faith in God. The ultimate word about the future does not rest with human oppressors, such as Sennacherib of Assyria or any of his successors. Human rulers of the people of God should not forget God's sovereignty. They should be like the pious and trusting Hezekiah, and not like his predecessors. But beyond these generalities, deciding how the composers intended the story to be heard is difficult.

Did they mean to imply that Jerusalem was forever secure from foreign invasion? Some persons in Judah were confident of that (2 Samuel 7:4-16; Jeremiah 7:1-4; 26:7-11; Psalms 89:1-4; 132:11-18). Such a conclusion can be derived from Isaiah 36–37 only by analogy, however: Just as God delivered the sacred city from Sennacherib, so we trust that God will deliver it from the Assyrians at present.

Those who read the corresponding chapters in Second Kings would have been less likely to make such an analogy. There, the history of Judah continues beyond the reign of Hezekiah, and he is succeeded by the evil King Manasseh. The security of the city erodes, and prophets announce its impending destruction (2 Kings 21:10-15). We should not be surprised, therefore, that the later Babylonians succeeded in doing what the Assyrians could not. Does the story in Kings suggest that this destruction would not have

73

happened had the rulers been as willing to trust God as had Hezekiah?

Which of the following do you think is the more appropriate reaction? (1) These chapters contain an interesting, and perhaps valid, interpretation of the Assyrian invasion. But that single event is long past, and we do not live in Jerusalem. The passage promises no security for any other spot and time. We may, however, learn something about God's control of history, and admire the faith of Hezekiah. (2) Although we do not live in Jerusalem, we can learn something about the source of security that is beyond all others. We ought to trust in God, rather than in military weapons and political alliances. If we do so, we will be secure. (3) No amount of faith, or trust in God, is an absolute guarantee of political security for any group. However, we can learn something from this passage about God's control of history. If we lose our security, that too is within God's providence. We must try to learn from that experience, and start anew.

A MESSAGE OF DELIVERANCE

Isaiah 40–44

DIMENSION ONE: WHAT DOES THE BIBLE SAY?

Answer these questions by reading Isaiah 40

1. What encouraging words are now announced? (40:1-2)

2. What should the people do? (40:3-4, 11)

3. What type of terrain must be crossed in this journey? (40:3)

4. Who is the speaker in this chapter? (40:6)

5. Why should the hearers believe the message of forgiveness and deliverance? (40:8, 18, 28)

Answer these questions by reading Isaiah 41

6. Who is to bring about the deliverance that has been promised? (41:2)

7. Who is the speaker now? (41:4)

8. What are those who doubt that the deliverance will come challenged to do? (41:21)

Answer these questions by reading Isaiah 42

9. What will be accomplished by the servant? (42:1- 4)

10. What should the people do? (42:10)

11. What indicates that the speaker's audience does not believe the message? (42:16, 18, 19)

Answer these questions by reading Isaiah 43

12. What has prompted God to act on behalf of the Judeans? (43:4)

13. Where are the Judeans at this time? (43:5-6)

14. Rather than believing in a new future, what are the people doing? (43:18)

Answer these questions by reading Isaiah 44

15. What do idols do? (44:9)

16. What is the status of past sins? (44:22)

17. Once forgiveness and deliverance are believed to be possible, what will the hearers do? (44:23)

18. Who is the agent of God's deliverance? (44:28)

DIMENSION TWO: WHAT DOES THE BIBLE MEAN?

■ **Background.** Chapter 40 is a transition from prose to poetry. By now, you should be sensitive to such transitions. They account for a new or different audience or a new speaker.

The author of chapters 40–55 is called "Second Isaiah" by scholars. He comforts and encourages. The pointed condemnations that are associated with the prophet Isaiah are no longer to be seen. No longer is there a mixture of negative and positive speeches, caused by alternating of the speeches between Isaiah and his disciples. This section is purely positive in tone.

A major problem, as we read this material, is to know how it is arranged. These chapters could be one long speech, with development of thought from beginning to end. Or

GENESIS to REVELATION **ISAIAH**

they could be a series of small speeches, joined together in logical order. They could even be a series of small speeches with no coherent order, or a series of small speeches joined together by word-association. As illustrations of the last of these possibilities, notice how various sections of chapter 41 may be united by the phrase "Do not fear, I will help you" (vv. 10, 13, 14). In chapter 44, the terms *redeemed* and *Redeemer* are repeated in various sections (44:22, 23, 24).

Spaces between sections sometimes suggest a change in audience, or occasion, or topic. This section includes so many of these that they reduce the words of the prophet to fragments. Can some larger organization or line of argument be detected? It may be helpful to read each of the following sections as a "rhetorical unit":

- *Isaiah 40:1-11* presents a new religious situation. The previous period of judgment, caused by Judah's sin, is over! God now comes to save.
- *Isaiah 40:12-31* tells of the Lord's superiority over other gods and activity in history.
- *Isaiah 41:1-29* tells of the role of Cyrus the Persian in the Lord's plan. God's promise to help now begins to take concrete form.
- *Isaiah 42:1-13* discusses Israel's role in the new future. This section is difficult to understand.
- *Isaiah 42:14–43:13* tells of the exiles' deafness to their new role. The message falls on deaf ears because of the people's depression.
- *Isaiah 43:14–44:23* tells that the exiles' lack of response to the prophet's message is caused by a sense of unworthiness for past sins. Nonetheless, God will do a "new thing." The past must not be dwelled on.
- *Isaiah 44:24–45:13* reaffirms Cyrus as God's agent.

■ **Isaiah 40:2.** By using the word *double*, the prophet shows his agreement with the charge that the Exile is far more punishment than the people deserved.

■ **Isaiah 40:3.** The voice is a heavenly one, calling the prophet to his task. The first Isaiah also received a commission through a heavenly voice (6: 1-13). The highway will lead from Babylon back to Jerusalem.

■ **Isaiah 40:6.** A more accurate translation of "cry out" would be "announce."

■ **Isaiah 40:6-8.** This section is not well punctuated. The prophet wonders why he should announce comfort, since human life is of short duration and ends quickly, like the grass. This response reflects the pessimism of the exiles. Then, in verse 8, the heavenly voice responds that, by contrast, God's word that is now to be announced is eternally true. Thus, the prophet is to proclaim aloud (v. 9).

■ **Isaiah 40:12-31.** The Lord has overseen creation (vv. 12-17). No other gods maybe appealed to, or even exist (vv. 18-20). This has long been known in Israel and not a new message (vv. 21-26). Why should the exiles assume that their situation is unknown or hopeless (vv. 27-31)?

■ **Isaiah 40:19.** The Lord cannot be compared to those gods represented by idols, because humans made them.

■ **Isaiah 40:22.** The earth was thought to be flat like a circle.

■ **Isaiah 40:24.** "They" refers to the princes and rulers of verse 23. They soon wither, as will the rulers of Babylon who are now oppressing the exiles.

■ **Isaiah 40:26.** "These" refers to the stars.

■ **Isaiah 40:28.** The exiles assume that God has grown weary, so that the events of history are no longer a concern.

■ **Isaiah 41:1-29.** Let the world take note of what God is about to do (v. 1). God is behind the activity of a conspicuous military figure (vv. 2-7). This statement has implications for the exiles (vv. 8-20). Skeptics are challenged in verses 21-24. Verses 25-29 contain more information about the military figure.

■ **Isaiah 41:2.** The speaker, in good literary style, does not yet name the military figure. He lets tension build about him. The "he" who gives up nations to the military figure is the same as the "who" at the beginning of the verse. In verse

4, we learn that it is the Lord. Otherwise in the verse, the pronouns "he" and "him" refer to the military figure.

■ **Isaiah 41:6-7.** The transition in thought is a bit rough. In contrast to the Lord, "the first" and "the last" of verse 4, the other gods to whom the exiles might appeal are nothing more than the idols that worshipers make.

■ **Isaiah 41:15-16.** Possibly, the mountains and hills are those that will block the exiles' return to their homeland.

■ **Isaiah 41:17-20.** The desert that stretches between Babylonia and Canaan posed a barrier to travel. Travelers had to go around it by means of the Euphrates River valley. Filled with enthusiasm, the prophet indicates that the desert will not be a barrier to a quick and safe return home.

■ **Isaiah 41:21-24.** The exiles who have turned to other faiths are challenged to authenticate their gods. Can they explain the past and future, as the Lord's prophets have done? Can other gods affect history, as the Lord is about to do?

■ **Isaiah 41:25.** Cyrus's home is east of Babylonia (41:2), but his military activities have been to the northeast and north.

■ **Isaiah 41:26.** The "it" that was made known long ago is not the activity of Cyrus, as if the prophets were predictors of the future. Rather, it is the message of God's concern for Israel.

■ **Isaiah 42:1-13.** Who is this servant? No one knows for sure. Some scholars think it is Cyrus, since the previous verses (41:25-29) have praised Cyrus. *Servant* would be an appropriate title for Cyrus. God has summoned him and will anoint him for service (45:1). As a conqueror and empire builder, he might indeed be expected to bring justice to the nations and to free prisoners.

Since the exiles themselves are called God's servant throughout Second Isaiah, it would seem likely that they are meant here as well (41:8, 9; 42:19; 43:10; 44:1, 2, 21; 48:20). Like the servant, the exiles understood themselves to be God's chosen ones (43:10, 20; 44:1, 2). Possibly, they think of themselves as a potential source of illumination (42:6).

Other scholars feel the servant is Second Isaiah himself. He describes himself as God's servant in 49:5 and as one possessed of God's spirit (48:16). Indeed, this is the sort of title that a prophet would be expected to claim.

The prophet could also be predicting God's action, without having any specific agent in mind. The servant thus might be a future, ideal ruler anointed by God. Another possibility is that the servant is a future messiah. After all, the prophet's talk is to address the problems of the exiles in Babylonia and to tell them where God is amidst a perplexing present. But a vague, indefinite, future expectation would hardly be of comfort to them under the circumstances. The servant is described in the past and present tenses. He is already on the scene (42:4).

While one verse or another of 42:1-9 can be made to fit any one of these possibilities, it is difficult to see how the whole passage can support any one interpretation.

Another problem is that no one knows how many individual speeches are contained in 41:25–42:9. If there is only one speech, we would expect the servant to be the same throughout. But we cannot tell whether there is only one speech or more. Modern scholars are divided as to how many speeches there are and who the servant is.

■ **Isaiah 42:6.** The Hebrew expression behind "covenant for the people" is found elsewhere in the Bible only at Isaiah 49:8. What the phrase means is unclear. Look at several translations.

■ **Isaiah 42:7.** Ordinarily in the second Isaiah, the blind and the prisoners are the despondent exiles. If that is the case here, then who opens their eyes? The prophet, elsewhere, accepts that task for himself (49:4-6).

■ **Isaiah 42:14–43:13.** God repeats the promise of a new future (42:14-1 7), but the depressed exiles are unable to believe it (42:18-25), so renewed assurances are given (43:1-13).

■ **Isaiah 42:14.** The Exile has gone on for a long time, and some have wondered about the existence or power of God.

81

But now, at the appropriate time, God breaks the silence. God, like a woman in childbirth, now brings forth new life.

■ **Isaiah 42:15.** God's judgment, directed against the Babylonian oppressors, will affect nature.

■ **Isaiah 42:21.** God acts despite the exiles' blindness.

■ **Isaiah 42:24-25.** Since God has been responsible for such acts in the past, surely God has the power to act in the present.

■ **Isaiah 43:2.** The prophet, through poetic exaggeration, tries to encourage and prepare the exiles for the difficult trip home across rivers and deserts.

■ **Isaiah 43:14-23.** The despondent exiles want to dwell on the past, but God will do a new thing (43:14-21). Despite their previous failures (43:22-24), God will forgive and bless them anew (43:25; 44:8). Those who continue to worship idols are denounced (44:9-20), and the people are again exhorted to respond (44:21-22). In view of these events, the prophet breaks into song (44:23).

■ **Isaiah 43:16-17.** God's deliverance at the time of the Exodus is called to mind.

■ **Isaiah 43:18-19.** The deliverance from Egypt is more than an historical record. It provides the model for a new exodus in the present.

■ **Isaiah 43:27.** By "first father," the prophet likely means Jacob. He was given the group name Israel (see also 44:1, where the exiles are called Jacob).

■ **Isaiah 44:2.** Jeshurun is an ancient title for Israel. Its meaning is no longer clear.

■ **Isaiah 44:9-20.** This long section, sometimes set as prose (NRSV), is unexpected. Modern interpreters often consider it a later addition to the book. However, this passage contains a point of view similar to that of the prophet.

■ **Isaiah 44:15.** Only now does the speaker's point begin to emerge.

■ **Isaiah 44:18.** Such blindness on the part of idol makers can be attributed only to the true God.

■ **Isaiah 44:20.** The quotation is hard to understand. The REB translates it "This thing I am holding is a sham."

■ **Isaiah 44:24-28.** Since this speech opens a new topic, we will consider it with chapter 45 in the next lesson.

DIMENSION THREE: WHAT DOES THE BIBLE MEAN TO ME?

The Prophet's Audience

Before we discuss *what* the Bible means in the present, it may be well to think about *how* it means something. Who, do you think, was the prophet's original and intended audience? Was it those of his own generation who heard his words proclaimed with their own ears? If so, a problem arises. His intended audience is dead and gone. His words had their intended effect. What, then, does the passage say to us? But if the prophet's intended audience included generations yet unborn, was the message intended for us? Rather than giving advice to a specific situation in his own time, was he giving timeless advice?

What evidence in the Bible supports your opinion? What specific problem in the prophet's time needed to be addressed? Is a specific audience named? Is the prophet's language in the past, present, or future tense? What is the task of a prophet, as you understand it: to speak to the prophet's time, or to predict our time, or both?

To Whom Is Isaiah Speaking?

Also, before we discuss *what* the Bible means in the present, we may also need to think about *to whom* it should mean something. Which of the following do you think is more nearly correct? (1) When the prophet speaks to "you," as he often does, he is speaking to each reader. Each person may claim the promises for herself or himself. It would be entirely proper, then, to publish a collection of his promises under such topical headings as "What to Read When You Need Forgiveness," "What to Read When You Are Sick," "What to Read When You Are Lonely." (As a matter of fact, such volumes exist, but range over the entire Bible rather than being limited to our prophet). For example, one who is afraid might read 43:1-7 and find comfort.

(2) When the prophet speaks to "you," he has a collective audience in mind ("you all"). Thus, when he speaks of the intent "to free captives from prison / and to release from the dungeon those who sit in darkness" (42:7), he has an oppressed people in mind rather than depressed individuals.

If you choose option 2, to what groups should the prophet's words be addressed in the present: any group that is oppressed, or one specific group only? What was the nature of the prophet's initial audience? What is the equivalent of that audience today?

Why is it important for readers of the Bible to think about problems like this? Or are these issues important at all?

For the sake of Jacob my servant, / of Israel my chosen, /
I summon you by name. (45:4)

THE COMMISSION OF CYRUS

Isaiah 45–48

DIMENSION ONE: WHAT DOES THE BIBLE SAY?

Answer these questions by reading Isaiah 45

1. Why has God chosen Cyrus of Persia? (45:4, 6)

2. How do the exiles respond to the prophet's announcement about Cyrus? (45:9-11)

3. What is the exiles' response when they finally begin to grasp what it is that God has done through Cyrus? (45: 15)

4. What are those who survive Cyrus's destruction of Babylon to conclude? (45:22-24)

Answer these questions by reading Isaiah 46

5. How are the gods of the Babylonians contrasted with Israel's God? (46:1-4, 7)

6. What does God call Cyrus? (46:11)

Answer these questions by reading Isaiah 47

7. What reasons are given for God's anger against the Babylonians? (47:6)

8. What additional reason is given? (47:8)

9. On what have the Babylonians relied in order to secure their future? (47:12-13)

Answer these questions by reading Isaiah 48

10. Why has God spoken through the prophets? (48:5)

11. What will God do for the people? (48:6)

12. What has God done for Cyrus? (48:14-15)

13. What does the prophet remind the people of? (48:21)

DIMENSION TWO: WHAT DOES THE BIBLE MEAN?

■ **Background.** The various speeches contained in chapters 45–48 concentrate on a common theme: how God works for the salvation of Judah. God does not work through one of Judah's own number, but through a pagan foreigner, Cyrus of Persia. The audience finds that claim difficult to accept, and so the prophet argues strenuously in order to demonstrate its truth.

■ **Isaiah 44:24–45:13.** The "new thing" alluded to in 43:18-19 is now given concrete form. Cyrus is reaffirmed as the Lord's agent. Since God has "made all things" (44:24), the conclusion is inescapable. Cyrus is not acting on his own. God is acting, not merely for the sake of the exiles (45:4), but in order to convince others of divine sovereignty (45:6).

■ **Isaiah 45:1.** That the Lord might have sovereignty over a foreign king was believable. However, that God had anointed Cyrus, just as the descendants of David were said to be anointed, was surely a daring thing to say. The prophet was sure to provoke skepticism, which he does, in fact, encounter.

■ **Isaiah 45:7.** The Persians believed in two equal deities, one characterized by light and the other by darkness. The prophet may be denying their existence. The Judeans must reckon with only one divine force.

■ **Isaiah 45:9-11.** Presumably, the skeptical exiles have questioned the prophet's announcement in 44:24 and 45:8. He characterizes them as one who would argue with their Maker. He compares them to pots that would criticize the designer who brought them into being. Do they not realize that the Designer of history knows more than they?

■ **Isaiah 45:13.** The prophet ends where he began, with the call of Cyrus.

■ **Isaiah 45:14–46:13.** The Lord's uniqueness is now stressed. No one else could have summoned Cyrus. Unlike idolaters, who are confused by obscure prophecies (45:16-19) and whose gods cannot save them (45:20), the Lord declared the state of affairs long in advance (45:18-19). In contrast to idols, who must be carried by their worshipers and even saved by them (46:1-2, 6-7), the Lord undergirds and saves the exiles (46:3-4). When they remember other times of such salvation, the exiles should be more receptive to the new deliverance that is now announced (46:8-13).

■ **Isaiah 45:15.** Presumably, the exiles now make this statement. They seem finally to have realized that God works in mysterious ways, beyond their traditional expectations.

■ **Isaiah 45:16-17.** The prophet now resumes his speech.

■ **Isaiah 45:20.** The survivors may be the citizens of Babylon, after the conquest of that place by Cyrus. What, now, is to be the prophet's (and the exiles') attitude toward their former enemies? What is the Lord's stance toward the Babylonians? The answer is given in verses 22-23. They must now confess that there is no other God.

■ **Isaiah 46:1.** Bel and Nebo are Babylonian gods whose idols were carried about the city during religious festivals.

■ **Isaiah 46:34.** Unlike the Babylonian gods, who will be carried away by the conqueror, the Lord has sustained Judah even during the Exile. No stronger contrast between the two deities can be drawn.

■ **Isaiah 46:11.** The man from "a far-off land" is Cyrus.

■ **Isaiah 47:1-15.** All the prior announcements by the prophet now reach their goal. The bird of prey (46:11) now claims its victim, Babylon. Lest we feel pity for its inhabitants, justification is given for their fate. They have shown no mercy (47:6), have acted arrogantly (47:8), have indulged in wickedness (47:10), and practiced sorceries (47:12-13).

■ **Isaiah 47:1-2.** Who is the "Virgin Daughter of Babylon"? The NRSV translates the phrase as "virgin daughter Babylon," which is preferable. Babylon is like a young woman of high birth who is reduced to the rank of a slave. Formerly delicate, she must now perform menial tasks.

■ **Isaiah 47:6.** The period of God's anger is a reference to the Exile, which is now ended.

■ **Isaiah 47:8.** The words here attributed to Babylon are those the prophet often attributes to God (46:9). Thus, Babylon thinks of itself as a god (eternal, powerful, beyond challenge).

■ **Isaiah 47:9.** Sorceries and enchantments are religious rituals that were performed in order to ensure the stability and continuity of the state.

■ **Isaiah 47:13.** Astrologers divided the heavens into sections for the purpose of predicting the future. They wanted to help the state ensure its stability. In this passage, the prophet ridicules such efforts.

■ **Isaiah 48:1-22.** The exiles are reluctant to trust the prophet's words, because the words are so innovative. Why couldn't other prophets know that God would work in this fashion? Thus, a contrast is made between the long-standing declaration of "former things" (48:3-5) and the announcement of "new things" (48:6-11).

In each case, God's mode of operation was determined by the people's perverse nature. Had the past not been declared by the Lord's prophets, then the opinion of other gods would have been manufactured and proposed. The Lord shows that to be impossible. But now, a different way of doing things is necessary. Had the return from exile been announced long in advance, the people would have grown complacent. They would not be surprised at God's gracious action. They would have said, "I knew it all along!" In any case, only the Lord could have brought about the deliverance that is now at hand (48:12-16).

■ **Isaiah 48:14-16.** This section is filled with pronouns that have indefinite references. *Him* seems to be Cyrus, and *me* (v. 16) likely is the prophet.

■ **Isaiah 48:18.** The Exile need not have happened. The people brought it on themselves.

■ **Isaiah 48:21.** A parallel is drawn between the present and a previous return to the homeland. Just as God provided for the people at the time of the Exodus, so provision will now be made. The story in Exodus 17:1-7 is referred to.

■ **Isaiah 48:22.** This verse seems to be an editorial comment by a later reader. Such remarks are sometimes found at the end of a prophetic section. See 57:21 for the same remark.

DIMENSION THREE: WHAT DOES THE BIBLE MEAN TO ME?

God's Concern

One of the goals of the second Isaiah is to convince the exiles that God is still concerned about them. The prophet reminds them of terms that have described their status in the past. Among other things, they have been called "my people" (40:1), "my servant" (41:8; 42:19; 43:10; 44:1), "chosen" (41:8; 44:1), "my sons . . . my daughters" (43:6), and "called" (48:12). The community has been sustained by God from birth; it will be sustained in the present and future: "even to your old age" (46:4). The Exile does not contradict that reality, since God carries the community even now.

The prophet does not clearly spell out the reasons for God to continue to sustain the community, despite its failures that justified exile. The closest the prophet comes to an explanation is when he announces that God has acted "for my own [name's] sake" (48:9, 11). Only God knows the reasons that sustaining power is still granted, and why the community will be restored to its land. Whatever those reasons are, we can be certain that God desires the community to continue.

Some modern interpreters propose, rightly or wrongly, that part of God's intention (as the second Isaiah saw it) was that other groups came to realize God's sole sovereignty (45:14, 22, 23; 49:7). The miraculous continuation of Israel, despite all odds, would serve as compelling evidence of the claim, "I am the LORD, and there is no other" (45:5, 6).

The prophet's expectation may provide an occasion to discuss the continuation of the community in the present. (By *community*, I mean the church). Has the church, like its exilic predecessors, been guilty of failures that have contributed to its eclipse? What are some examples of the church's failures? Is the church an instrument for the wider recognition of God's sovereignty? Or is its effectiveness now diminished? Is it a viable institution, worthy of our commitments of time and money? How do our (my) actions display that conviction? The exiles' doubts about this matter made them despondent, unwilling to be active in their faith or to venture out to return home. Is that true of us? How can we turn that attitude around?

Who Is God?

Before the exiles would be convinced that there was a future for them, they first had to make a decision about God. Is there a single sovereign power in control of history, or are there many, more limited powers, we must come to terms with? Who is God? Is it Israel's Yahweh or Babylon's Bel (Marduk) and Nebo, or the twin gods of the Persians? How individuals of the Exile responded to the prophet's message of liberation depended on what or who they worshiped. The importance of this problem is reflected in the number of times that the prophet returns to it, and in the passion with which he discusses it (40:12-31; 41:2-4, 21-29; 42:23-25; 43:8-13, 25-28; 44:6-20; 45:5-8, 14-25; 46:1-11; 47:8; 48:12-13).

To modern readers, God's identity may be a non-issue. After all, those polytheistic Canaanites, Babylonians, and Persians are gone. We do not have the option, as did the exiles, of worshiping at First Church Marduk. The only thing left (in the Judeo-Christian West, at least), is "God." And, according to some polls, a very large percentage of Americans believe in the existence of God or a universal spirit.

Do you think the prophet would be more impressed with our "belief in God" than he was with that of the exiles? Does our belief result in concrete actions in a way that theirs did not? If so, how? Despite what the vast majority of Americans say when asked by pollsters if they believe in God, many of our actions on an average weekday suggest something else. Is it possible to believe in God in theory, but be an atheist in practice? What actions would result from such an attitude?

We do not have the temptations and options that the ancient polytheists had; we must be either theist, atheist, or possibly agnostic. How do you react to this statement? Is it possible for us to worship gods without giving them names or even being aware that we are deifying them? What do you think might be some modern equivalents of Marduk (Bel) of Babylon? What might be the modern equivalents of the Canaanite god of fertility (Baal)?

For the LORD comforts his people, /and will have compassion on his afflicted ones. (49:13)

10
THE RESTORATION OF ZION

Isaiah 49–52; 54–55

DIMENSION ONE: WHAT DOES THE BIBLE SAY?

Answer these questions by reading Isaiah 49

1. What is the servant's evaluation of his activity? (49:4)

2. What is God's response to the servant's sense of failure? (49:6)

3. What is the response of the people of Zion to the possibility that the exiles may return home? (49:14)

4. Whereas Judah now is sparsely populated, what will the situation soon be? (49:20-21)

Answer these questions by reading Isaiah 50

5. What charge have the people brought against God because of the Exile? (50:1)

6. Whom does God hold responsible for the Exile? (50:1)

7. How have the exiles treated God's messenger? (50:6)

8. What is the speaker's response to rejection? (50:7)

Answer these questions by reading Isaiah 51

9. What past event does the prophet tell about here? (51:1-2)

10. How long will the promised deliverance last? (51:6, 8)

11. How are the exiles described? (51:17, 19, 21)

Answer this question by reading Isaiah 52

12. How will nations and kings react when they realize what God has done for the servant? (52:14-15)

Answer these questions by reading Isaiah 54

13. With what is the exiled community compared? (54:1)

14. What bright future is painted for the community? (54:2-3)

15. The commitment God now makes is compared to what promise from Israel's past? (54:9-10)

Answer these questions by reading Isaiah 55

16. With what is the worship of other gods compared? (55:1-2)

17. With whom is this new covenant made? (55:3)

DIMENSION TWO: WHAT DOES THE BIBLE MEAN?

■ **Background.** Isaiah 49:1-26. This section contains God's promises to Zion. God's servant discusses his role in verses 1-6. The response of neighboring peoples to the release of the exiles is described in verse 7. Verses 8-12 tell about the return to the land of Canaan. Verse 13 is a hymn of thanksgiving. Verses 14-26 describe the doubts of the residents of Zion, and their subsequent reassurance.

■ **Isaiah 49:1-6.** The second of the so-called Servant Songs is surrounded by almost as much obscurity and controversy as was the previous one (see the note to 42:1-13). While Cyrus the Persian is not a very likely candidate here, it may be argued that this servant is either the prophet or the community.

■ **Isaiah 49:7.** The traditional beginning formula, "This is what the LORD says," suggests that a new speech or topic begins here. The subject is now clearly the exiles. They were despised by their neighbors (Psalm 137:1-3) and are now servants of the king of Babylon. But when the power of the Lord is revealed at the exiles' release, the nations will prostrate themselves before the Lord (45:14, 23; 52:15).

■ **Isaiah 49:8.** Whoever the "you" is, it is clear that God's purpose in acting is to reestablish the land of Canaan, to repopulate its desolate cities, and to free the exiles. The thought that the scattered Judeans will return to their homeland from lands afar continues in verse 12.

■ **Isaiah 49:16.** God has arranged a constant reminder of the exiles' plight. Human beings were sometimes branded in the palm as a reminder of their status as slaves. God is so branded.

■ **Isaiah 49:18.** The "you" who is addressed is apparently Mount Zion in Jerusalem. "Them" refers to the exiles.

■ **Isaiah 49:24.** The "plunder" is the exiles. The "warriors" is Babylonia.

■ **Isaiah 49:26.** The nature and purpose of God's victory is made clear here. For related thoughts, see 45:14, 22-23; 49:7.

■ **Isaiah 50:1-11.** Although verses 1-3 and 4-11 are separate speeches, they may be studied together because they share the common theme of rejection by the community. In verses 1-3, it is God whom they reject; thereafter, it is the servant.

■ **Isaiah 50:1-2.** The deity's response presupposes that the people have accused God of abandoning them, as if a divorce decree had gone into effect. The preexilic prophets used such language to describe the deteriorating relationship between God and the people (see, for example, Hosea 2:1-7). Continuing that analogy, God responds that, if the relationship became strained, it was because of the people's iniquities and transgressions.

■ **Isaiah 50:2.** Justification for the Exile continues. God has called for repentance, but there was no meaningful response. But the situation is not beyond remedy. The exiles should not assume that God cannot, or will not, restore the relationship as it once was.

■ **Isaiah 50:4-9.** Although this section does not contain the word *servant*, this is the third of the Servant Songs in Second Isaiah. The word does occur, however, in 50:10-11. (For the other songs, see 42:1-9; 49:1-6). Interpreters have been divided over the identity of the servant here, as they were in the previous songs (see notes to 42:1-13; 49:1-6). Is the servant here the prophet or a faithful segment among the exiles, rejected by the skeptical majority?

■ **Isaiah 50:6.** The exiles doubt God's concern and power. Perhaps they fear that the prophet's announcement of Cyrus's victory over Babylon will arouse suspicions of treason. So the exiles have responded to the servant with derision and physical abuse. The speaker accepts the abuse and forges ahead. Suffering seems to have been accepted as part of the prophetic task.

■ **Isaiah 50:9.** The exiles should not assume, because their abuse of the servant goes unanswered, that the servant is wrong.

■ **Isaiah 50:10-11.** These verses, while perhaps not part of the Servant Song, are closely related to it. The servant no longer speaks of himself, but addresses the people. The exiles are exhorted to respond favorably to the servant, rather than to abuse him. Those who reject him are condemned with strong language (v. 11). The meaning of these verses is not entirely clear, however.

■ **Isaiah 51:1-8.** Assurance of God's deliverance is given in three related verses, each beginning with an imperative such as "Hear me" or "Listen."

■ **Isaiah 51:2.** Abraham, who was once in Babylonia, could reach the land of promise on his own, only as the result of God's initiative. So how much more hope should the entire community have.

■ **Isaiah 51:5.** The passage contains a number of related, perhaps parallel, expressions. But the meaning of "my arm will bring justice to the nations" is not parallel. In the NRSV, that phrase reads, "my arms will rule the peoples," which seems related to 45:22-23; 49:7, 23. Thus, by *salvation* the prophet apparently means God's victory over Babylon, when Israel triumphs over the enemies.

■ **Isaiah 51:6.** The text actually means that, whatever the duration of heaven and earth, God's deliverance will be even more enduring.

■ **Isaiah 51:9–52:15.** Three related speeches, each beginning with a double imperative (51:9; 51:17; 52:1), may be studied together. Their encouragement becomes increasingly strong, leading to the command to "depart, depart" (52:11).

■ **Isaiah 51:9-16.** A plea by the people for deliverance, citing God's actions in the past (vv. 9-10), brings God's answer (vv. 12-16). Verse 11, nearly identical to 35:10, does not neatly fit the scheme.

■ **Isaiah 51:10.** The Exodus from Egypt is recalled.

■ **Isaiah 51:12.** "Fear mortals" apparently refers to the Babylonian oppressors.

■ **Isaiah 51:14.** "The cowering prisoners" refers to the exiles.

■ **Isaiah 51:17-23.** A description of the depressed Judeans (vv. 17-20) leads to God's response (vv. 21-23). The description may be a paraphrase of a lament that the people recite (as is the case in 51:9-11).

■ **Isaiah 52:1-15.** This final section is confusing. The progression of thought may be as follows: Prepare to change from mourning to celebration (vv. 1-6), sing in anticipation of God's festive return to the holy city (vv. 7-10), prepare to depart (vv. 11-12), the nations will be astonished (vv. 13-15).

■ **Isaiah 52:1.** The words "uncircumcised and defiled" refer to the conquerors, who will no longer come to Jerusalem.

■ **Isaiah 52:3-6.** The transition to prose in some translations (see NRSV) is surprising, and the transition in thought is not smooth. Some interpreters suspect that this is an addition to Second Isaiah's speech. In any case, a motivation for God's deliverance of the exiles is offered. God will deliver them in order that the people may know who is God.

■ **Isaiah 52:7-10.** These verses proclaim news of release from exile. A messenger runs ahead and is spotted by guards as he approaches Jerusalem.

■ **Isaiah 52:11-12.** The entire message of the prophet now reaches its climax. In contrast to the Exodus, this one will not be a hasty flight.

■ **Isaiah 52:13-15.** The release of the exiles, who have been oppressed for decades, will be a source of astonishment among the peoples of the Near East. A similar thought is found in 49:7.

■ **Isaiah 54:1-17.** Rather than a mere promise of deliverance, the subject is now the new situation the people of Judah will find themselves in. This prophecy seems to advance beyond the previous speeches. A number of images of similar theme have been joined together. The formerly barren society will be blessed with offspring (vv. 1-3). The one alienated from her husband (God) will be restored, never to be alienated again (vv. 4-10). Wealth and security will abound (vv. 11-17). The overall result is more than a return to the "good old days." The new salvation is not conditional. Exile is not a future possibility.

■ **Isaiah 54:3.** The desolate cities are those that the Babylonians destroyed at the time of the Exile.

■ **Isaiah 54:11-14.** This poetic anticipation of the splendor of the renewed Jerusalem may be the inspiration for Revelation 21:10-21.

■ **Isaiah 55:1-13.** This chapter is made up of several speeches. They have been artfully combined into a fitting conclusion of all the second Isaiah's thought.

■ **Isaiah 55:1.** The model for this invitation to a new self-understanding may have been the feast that Near Eastern monarchs announced as part of their coronations. The royal subjects are summoned to hear the benefits to be bestowed on them during the new era.

■ **Isaiah 55:2.** Perhaps the Babylonian culture and its religion are the bread that "does not satisfy." Instead, they are offered that which will restore meaning to their lives (v. 3).

■ **Isaiah 55:3.** The covenant once made with the Davidic line is now extended to the entire people. The former mode of covenant ended at the Exile. The entire community is now a royal people.

■ **Isaiah 55:4.** What was to be accomplished through the monarchy will now be accomplished without it. This proposal is astonishing, in view of the role that kings had long played in Judean life. The kings claimed unending divine support (2 Samuel 7). Facing the future without royal leadership must have filled the exiles with anxiety.

■ **Isaiah 55:6-7.** This is not a general call to "whoever will." The call is intended for the exiles who have forsaken the traditional faith during their stay in Babylonia. It is a continuation of the invitation extended in verse 1.

■ **Isaiah 55:8-9.** God's "thoughts" are the plan to restore the exiles to their homeland. Such a possibility may have been beyond their comprehension and belief, but God's plans soar above those of humans. These ideas echo those of chapter 40.

■ **Isaiah 55:10-11.** These verses are not so much a general statement of God's reliability as an encouragement in the present circumstances. "The purpose for which I sent it" is the new mode of covenant outlined in verse 3, which presupposes a return to the Promised Land. This proposal is prefaced, in verses 1 and 6, by an invitation. God is offering an opportunity that may be either accepted or rejected. However, the prophet has faith that the offer will be accepted.

■ **Isaiah 55:12-13.** These verses are a final reminder of the prophet's major theme. In verse 13, the emphasis shifts from what is to be done to the one who acts. Judah should not view this event with vindication or self-satisfaction, but with praise to God.

DIMENSION THREE: WHAT DOES THE BIBLE MEAN TO ME?

Isaiah 55:1-5—A New Self-Understanding

When we read the prophet's vision of the community after its return from exile, we may be astonished to read that the Davidic monarchy that had ruled Judah for five hundred years apparently has to come to an end. Israel believed that God granted that office to David and his descendants unconditionally and for time without end (2 Samuel 7:8-17). The exiles must have been utterly astonished, then, when they heard the prophet announce the words in this passage. The people probably concluded that God was failing to keep a promise that had been firmly made.

In the understanding of the second Isaiah, God was changing tactics. God was going to act in a new way. God would not merely deliver the people from exile (43:18-19), but would redefine the covenant with David (55:3-4).

Where else in the Bible has God taken a new and unexpected direction in dealing with the believing community or even with the world? When in post-biblical times has God acted in this way? When in recent days? What are possible responses of human beings to changes in the world around them? What are some positive and negative aspects of change? What responsibilities fall on the believing community, in view of the biblical idea that God may abandon a long-standing approach and move in a new and unexpected direction?

The very nature of the "new" thing must have startled the exiles. The purpose of kingship, at its inception, had been to ensure justice within and security from without (1 Samuel 9:15-17; 2 Samuel 7:10-11, 16). The king was a visible sign of God's covenant. Without him, Israel's ability to know God's will, to formulate policy, to act decisively, and to be secure would be radically diminished. The people would be on their own, amidst the hostile forces of history.

The prophet's expectations were realized when, following the Exile, the monarchy was rejected in favor of priestly leadership. But not everyone agreed with the change. Some thought that in the future, surely a descendant of David must arise. This person would be a hero-messiah, who would end the ambiguities of history and usher in the era of divine rule. The present community, even with God's blessing, could not sufficiently "witness to the peoples" such that "nations you do not know you will come running to you" (Isaiah 55:4-5).

Throughout its history, the church has alternated between periods of optimistic outreach ("The kingdom of God is here and now in the ministry of the church; Christ is among us") and periods of pessimistic withdrawal ("The kingdom of God is not of this world; Christ is coming soon"). At times, the expectations of the second Isaiah seemed to be well-founded. God's power and the presence of the Spirit were sufficient for continuation and success. At other times, such goals and power have seemed insufficient. A heavenly king must appear and save us!

Are these two points of view still operative in the church today? How are these ideas reflected in your congregation? Is it important that both ideas be maintained, or is only one of them right? What are the merits and dangers of each point of view?

Surely he took up our pain / and bore our suffering, / yet we considered him punished by God, / stricken by him, and afflicted. (53:4)

11
THE SUFFERING SERVANT

Isaiah 53

DIMENSION ONE:
WHAT DOES THE BIBLE SAY?

Answer these questions by reading Isaiah 53

1. Do the speakers describe a future event, or one that has already come to pass? (53:1-3)

2. Who is described in this chapter? (53:2, 11)

3. Who are the observers and speakers in this chapter? (53:1, 8)

4. What is the spiritual condition of those who speak? (53:6)

5. Is there evidence the servant was subject to a trial? (53:8)

6. How do we know that God is now the speaker? (53:8)

7. What evidence is there that mention of "cut off from the land of the living," "grave," and "death" in 53:8-9 do not describe physical death? (53:10-11)

8. What evidence is there that "we" are again the speakers? (53:10)

9. How do we know that God again responds? (53:11-12)

DIMENSION TWO: WHAT DOES THE BIBLE MEAN?

■ **Background.** Chapter 53 of Isaiah merits an entire lesson. This chapter is filled with unique and ambiguous expressions that require much discussion in order to understand them. The early church understood the mission of Jesus in the light of this chapter, and sometimes suggested that Jesus understood himself in its light. Modern interpreters often propose that the suffering servant of this passage is the proper model for the church.

Certain features of these passages led scholars to propose that the servant who is described in them has a separate identity. He is not the same servant who appears elsewhere in Second Isaiah, representing the exiled community. Who is this special servant? No one person would easily "fit" all four descriptions. Since the figure seemed to suffer (in chaps. 50; 53), and since God addressed him as "my servant" (42:1; 49:3; 53:11), modern interpreters have designated him the Suffering Servant or the Servant of the Lord.

A number of interesting identities for this servant have been suggested, among them various monarchs and a resurrected Moses. In general, Jewish interpreters have understood the servant as collective Israel (the exiles). In general, Christian interpreters have understood the servant of these texts either as a future messiah or as an ideal Israel within the larger body, a faithful remnant (based primarily on 49:3, 5).

A minority of modern interpreters has rightly maintained that the second Isaiah is the author of these four songs. Furthermore, while it is true that the word *servant* does not mean *Israel* as it does elsewhere in chapters 40–55, a single identification will not fit all the songs. Such a false assumption has led to most of the difficulty that modern interpreters have encountered in identifying the servant.

We have seen so far that in 42:1-4, no secure identification can be drawn. In 49:1-6, the servant is probably the prophet himself. In 50:4-9, the servant is surely the prophet himself. The identification of the servant in Isaiah 53 has been discussed since New Testament times. In Acts 8:34, the Ethiopian eunuch asks Philip, "Tell me, please, who is the prophet talking about, himself or someone else?" Philip then tells him about Jesus. Exactly what connection Philip proposes between the servant and Jesus is not said. Later, some interpreters within the church assumed that there was a point-by-point correspondence between the servant and Jesus. Thus expressions like "we held him in low esteem" (v. 3), "punished by God" (v. 4), "cut off from the land of the living" (v. 8), "assigned a grave with the wicked" (v. 9), and "prolong his days" (v. 10) suggest that the prophet had predicted the life, death, and resurrection of Jesus. Assumed parallels between the two figures led to an understanding of the servant as a vicarious figure (that is, someone who suffers as an innocent substitute for ones who are guilty). The following descriptions of the servant seemed to support that portrait: "took up our pain" (v. 4), "pierced for our transgressions

. . . / the punishment that brought us peace . . . / by his wounds we are healed" (v. 5), "laid on him / the iniquity of us all" (v. 6), "will bear their iniquities" (v. 11), and "he poured out his life unto death / . . . bore the sin of many, / and made intercession for the transgressors" (v. 12).

Many phrases in this chapter are unique to Isaiah, and their meanings are ambiguous. Some modern translations may have been influenced by the assumed connections between Jesus and the servant. In these cases, Christian ideas have been "read back" into the text of Isaiah. Our first task is to understand the prophet as he meant to be understood in his own time and context.

Defining where this fourth song begins is crucial. Usually, modern interpreters have assumed that the starting point is 52:13, "See, my servant will act wisely; / he will be raised and lifted / up and highly exalted." Many nations and kings are then startled because of what happens to the servant (52:15). The nations then begin to speak at 53:1, "Who has believed our message?" This verse might be suggesting that the servant is to have an impact on the world. In that case, the following possible identifications of the servant would seem to fit. (1) The servant, as in the rest of chapters 40–55, is the exiled community itself. God has called it to suffer, as a means of attracting attention to the true faith. This might be contrasted with what the prophet has said previously, that God's victory through Cyrus will force the rest of the world to conclude that God is with Israel alone, and thus "they will trudge behind you, coming over to you in chains" (45:14). Thus, Israel would have discovered a new mission, a new mode of action in the world. (2) The servant might also be a future individual whose identity the prophet did not know. The messianic figure would embody true understanding and obedience to God, and bring others to new understanding (52:15).

However, the song does not necessarily begin at 52:13. Lesson 11 assumes that it begins, instead, at 53:1. If so, the speaker in that verse is not the "many nations and kings" of 52:15, and the servant in chapter 53 is not creating an impression on outsiders. No longer is the servant in chapter 53 the exiled community.

■ **Isaiah 53:1.** A report has reached a group, who now responds to it with a communal poetic chant. The report results in astonishment that such an event could have happened. No hint is given as to who *we* refers to, except that they apparently are worshipers of the Lord.

■ **Isaiah 53:2.** The identity of "he" is not stated, as if we knew him well. The meaning of the words "before him" is unclear. In context, the phrase appears to refer to the Lord. Perhaps he is someone the Lord has nurtured and of whom the Lord has expectations. The comparison with "a root out of dry ground" is also not entirely clear. Perhaps "he" is someone who has encountered difficulties from his surroundings. The remainder of the verse stresses that this was an ordinary-looking person. Nothing in his appearance would single him out as one chosen for divine service. The words have the ring of an excuse for not having recognized him for what he turned out to be.

■ **Isaiah 53:3.** "By mankind" is an overstatement. He was rejected by the community. The speaker in 50:6 was similarly mistreated by his contemporaries.

■ **Isaiah 53:4.** The meaning of "took up our pain / and bore our suffering" is unclear. Has the person suffered in place of us for our sins in general? Has he shared the griefs of the exiles in an intense fashion? Has he suffered because of the abuse caused by his message? The latter idea suggests that the sufferer is the prophet.

■ **Isaiah 53:5.** Again, the meaning is ambiguous. The verse could read "he was wounded as the result of our transgressions." If this is the case, what was it that we did that placed him in this dangerous situation? Has he been arrested, as verses 7-8 suggest? Precisely how this suffering is to affect our "peace" is not stated. If "we" are the exiled community, then any lack of well-being would be the result of the Exile itself. Then the servant's activity, for which he received corporal punishment, was directed toward our restoration. Perhaps the people who were once unwilling to be healed by listening to Isaiah (6:10) now realize that the second Isaiah was working to restore them.

■ **Isaiah 53:6.** Having "gone astray" is a good description of sinful Israel. This tendency eventually resulted in exile. The Hebrew expression translated as "laid on him the iniquity" occurs nowhere else in the Bible, and its meaning is far from clear. The verb does not mean to lay on in the sense of transfer, but can mean to reach, or to encounter. The phrase could possibly mean that his activity at God's bidding has caused our punishment to be extended to him. The word *iniquity* may be misleading, since the word can also mean punishment. He, then, has suffered punishment because of us.

■ **Isaiah 53:7-8.** These verses describe a judicial situation. The New Jerusalem Bible (NJB) translates verse 8 as "Forcibly, after sentence, he was taken. / Which of his contemporaries was concerned / at his having been cut off from the land of the living, / at his having been struck dead / for his people's rebellion?"

The expression "cut off from the land of the living" need not imply that the servant suffered physical death. Rather, the phrase is sometimes used to describe exclusion from human society. See 2 Chronicles 26:21, where the leprous King Uzziah is excluded from Temple worship because of his disease (the same verb is used in both places). In the Bible, the terms *life* and *death* are often used in a metaphoric sense rather than a biological one. *Life* is meaningful existence. *Death* is what detracts from life as God intended it.

The expression "my people" is surprising. We expect the same speakers to continue. But now, beginning in verse 7, statements are made from the perspective of God. Perhaps the exiles have been the ones speaking previously as "we . . . our." Thus, "my people" in this verse would be different from "my servant" in verse 11. The exiles are not the servant.

■ **Isaiah 53:9.** That the servant did not die is clear from verses 10-12. To be "assigned a grave" means that he was regarded as being as good as dead, or written off. The REB reads, "He was assigned a grave with the wicked, / a burial-place among felons."

■ **Isaiah 53:10.** "We" begin to speak again, following God's words in verses 7-9. The Hebrew expression behind "the LORD makes his life an offering for sin" is unique in the Bible. Both its syntax and vocabulary are obscure.

Whatever the nature of his suffering, the servant apparently survives and lives a long life with his children. The prophet has probably been released from prison and now enjoys divine blessings. The word *offspring* is never used in any sense other than physical, biological descendants. So the word does not mean spiritual followers.

■ **Isaiah 53:11.** The words "my righteous servant" suggest that God is again the speaker, perhaps beginning at "by his knowledge." The author cannot have meant that the suffering of the servant will "justify" (NIV) sinners, or "make many righteous" (NRSV). According to God's own instructions to Israel, such an action (acquitting the guilty) was a heinous act (Proverbs 17:15; Isaiah 5:23). Perhaps he will use his prophetic teaching to help the people become righteous. That has been the second Isaiah's goal all along. The last phrase of the verse has a parallel in Lamentations 5:7, "Our ancestors sinned and are no more; / and we bear their punishment." That is, we suffer as a consequence of the mistaken political policies of our ancestors. The present passage may mean that the servant suffers as a consequence of the exiles' acts and attitudes. According to 50:6, they physically abused him. Perhaps they reported him to the Babylonian authorities. In any case, they seem to have regarded his fate as justified (53:4)

■ **Isaiah 53:12.** The expression behind "poured out his life unto death" does not mean actual biological death. As we have seen, the servant will live a long life in the presence of his descendants (v. 10). The passage means he exposed himself to death. They may have known when he spoke of Babylon's coming defeat at the hands of Persia, that he risked execution by the Babylonian authorities. He would be reckoned by them as a rebel ("numbered with the transgressors").

The expression "bore the sin of many" probably means the same as verse 11, "he will bear their iniquities." The idea is that the servant shares the burden of their punishment as a fellow exile. Now he suffers even more as a consequence of his audience's rebellious actions. Despite their doubts of his message and even their physical abuse of him (50:6), he has interceded (prayed) for them.

In view of the notes above, the portrait of the servant that emerges is consistent with that of 49:1-6 and 50:4-9. In the two previous passages, the servant appeared to be the second Isaiah himself. In those passages, the prophet, believing that God has sent him to "bring Jacob [the exiles] back to him" (49:5), feels that he has been a failure. The people would not listen to him (49:4). They have physically abused the prophet (50:6), but he has persisted in his message (50:7). And his audience, questioning his call and perhaps fearing reprisal from the Babylonian government, "hide their faces" from him (53:3). The people see nothing in his appearance to commend him as God's spokesman (53:2).

As one of the exiles, and as the result of his prophetic mission, he not only suffers with them; he also suffers as a consequence of their faithlessness. Little did they realize that his announcements and persistence were for their well-being (53:4-6). The Babylonians saw the servant's stance as seditious. Perhaps they even considered him to be a spy. Not surprisingly, they arrested, tried, and sentenced him to prison (53:7-8). To the exiles, these actions only served as proof that his words had no validity. The servant was now cut off, done for, as good as dead (53:9). And then, amazingly, the prophet apparently was released. Who could have believed such a thing (53:1)? At last, it is evident that he is God's servant, deserving life and blessing (53:10-12).

DIMENSION THREE: WHAT DOES THE BIBLE MEAN TO ME?

The Servant of the Lord

What Isaiah 53 will mean to readers within the church in the present will depend, to a large extent, on how they identify the servant who is mentioned in it.

1. Those who identify the servant with a future person, the Messiah, will marvel at how accurately the prophet predicted the ministry of Jesus, some five hundred fifty years in advance. The chapter thus becomes a monument to prophetic abilities. Some interpreters who hold this view have proposed that the servant might become a model for individual behavior in the present. Such a servant voluntarily suffers for others.

2. Those who have identified the servant with the exiled community have usually proposed that the servant is a model for the church in the present. Interpreters have proposed that the exiled, because of their willingness to trust God and risk the trip home, have incited the interest of nearby nations and kings. They have led others to a new understanding of God. The church is encouraged to be a servant for those who have no power in the world. The church should suffer for the sake of justice and be an advocate for those without advocates.

3. If we identify the servant with the prophet himself, then readers in the church at present will not speak of our mission to anyone, since we are not the successors of the servant. Rather, we would see ourselves as the continuation of those to whom the servant was sent! We are those to whom God continues to send messengers.

Based on your study of Isaiah 53, what message does this chapter have for you? Who do you think the servant represents? How does the identity of the servant affect the chapter's meaning for us?

"The Redeemer will come to Zion, / to those in Jacob who repent of their sins." (59:20)

12

RESTORATION AND DISILLUSIONMENT

Isaiah 56–59

DIMENSION ONE: WHAT DOES THE BIBLE SAY?

Answer these questions by reading Isaiah 56

1. On what does the revealing of God's salvation depend? (56:1)

2. Who can become members of the community? (56:6-7)

3. What are the watchmen and shepherds doing? (56:10-12)

Answer these questions by reading Isaiah 57

4. Rather than worshiping the Lord, to whom have many of the people turned? (57:9)

5. What evidence is there that adversity, attributed to God's judgment, has already befallen the community? (57:16-17)

Answer these questions by reading Isaiah 58

6. What attests to the religious nature of the people? (58:2-3)

7. What indicates that their devotion to God is incomplete? (58:3-4)

8. What indicates that Jerusalem has not yet been rebuilt? (58:12)

Answer these questions by reading Isaiah 59

9. What charges have the people brought against God? (59:1)

10. Why has God been silent and inactive? (59:2)

11. What do the people say? (59:12)

12. What will God do for those who repent? (59:20)

DIMENSION TWO: WHAT DOES THE BIBLE MEAN?

■ **Background.** Many interpreters have suspected that there is a transition of some sort between chapters 55 and 56 of Isaiah. As you read chapters 56–59, see if you can detect the reasons for this suspicion. Do the prophet's concerns change? Do you see a change in attitude toward non-Judeans? Is there a change in speaker?

Some interpreters emphasize the transition and suspect a new prophetic voice. They have generally called this new voice Third Isaiah. Third Isaiah was probably a disciple of the second Isaiah. Perhaps he was responsible for editing the works of Second Isaiah.

Some commentators speak of a group rather than an individual disciple. Since the material is so diverse in literary form, emphases, and possible historical allusions, perhaps these chapters are a collection that was put together over a century or more. Most of the speeches can be dated to the period between the return from exile in Babylonia (539 BC) and the reform of Nehemiah (445 BC).

A few interpreters deemphasize the transition between chapters 55 and 56. They allow the second Isaiah's speeches to continue across that border. That interpretation would still allow for a change of location, mood, and emphases.

Your appreciation of these writings will be enhanced by an understanding of the situation of the exiles upon their return to Judea. In 539 BC, Cyrus, king of Persia, defeated the Babylonians and allowed the exiles to return home (2 Chronicles 36:22-23; Ezra 1:1-4). For many who chose to return at this time, it appeared that the message of the second Isaiah had been vindicated. Preexilic ambitions, goals, and mentalities were revived. Some of the exiles hoped that the Davidic monarchy could be restored. Perhaps the Temple could be rebuilt. Perhaps things would be just as they were before the Exile.

Reality was far removed from expectation, however. The Persians incorporated Judea into their empire, and hopes of independence were dashed. Restoration of the monarchy, with its nationalistic overtones, was also discouraged by the Persians. Even some of the Judeans thought that renewal of kingship would be a bad idea. The kings often had been corrupt and had even persecuted the prophets. Some Jews thought perhaps other forms of government should be instituted, provided the Persians would allow it. But what should the government be: elders, judges, priests of various types (Levites, Zadokites, Aaronites)? Factionalism was the order of the day.

The returning exiles were not greeted warmly by everyone in Judah. The exiles wanted their real estate back. They were a strain on the local economy. They tried to take over positions of leadership. Legal disputes must have been a common occurrence.

Foundations for rebuilding the Temple were laid (Ezra 5:14-16). But finances were limited and internal bickering slowed down the progress. Then, in 522 BC, King Cambyses of Persia died. His death kindled hopes of revolt and independence throughout the empire. This event may have encouraged the Judean prophets, Haggai and Zechariah, to press for the completion of the Temple and to anticipate that a new age was about to dawn. By 515 BC, the Temple was completed.

Widespread disillusionment led many citizens to worship the gods they had encountered in Babylonia. Others worshiped the gods of their pagan Judean neighbors. Some of the pious were increasingly dissatisfied with the present religious leadership. They looked increasingly to the future for a divinely inspired new age. The author (or authors) of chapters 56–66 seems to have belonged to such a visionary group.

For convenience and clarity of reading, this lesson may be divided as follows: (1) an admonition to observe the Sabbath (56:1-2); (2) the inclusiveness of the community (56:3-8); (3) criticism of leaders and cultic practices (56:9–57:13); (4) an announcement of impending salvation (57:14-21); (5) fasting defined as service that is pleasing to God (58:1-14); (6) accusation, contrition, and impending deliverance (59:1-21).

■ **Isaiah 56:3-8.** Keeping the Sabbath now becomes a crucial religious obligation. Prior to the Exile, the Sabbath had been observed, but it was not given a central place in religious identity.

■ **Isaiah 56:1-2.** A movement to exclude foreigners from worship seems to have gained strength after the Exile. This idea reached its zenith at the time of Ezra and Nehemiah. Such a tendency was counter to the expectations of the second Isaiah. He believed that foreigners would come to recognize that the Lord alone was God (Isaiah 45:14, 22-23; 49:7, 23). The alienation that foreigners now feel is expressed in verse 3, "Let no foreigner who is bound to the LORD say. . . ."

■ **Isaiah 56:3.** The mention of eunuchs is especially significant and shows the radical nature of the prophet's proposal. Deuteronomy contains a law that excluded eunuchs from Israel's worship (Deuteronomy 23:1-8).

■ **Isaiah 56:9–57:13.** These judgment speeches sound very much like those of the first Isaiah. They are a significant departure from the lyrical announcements of salvation found in the second Isaiah (chaps. 40–55).

■ **Isaiah 56:10-11.** "Watchmen" and "shepherds" are terms for leaders in the speeches of Jeremiah (6:17) and Ezekiel (3:17; 34:2).

■ **Isaiah 57:1.** "No one takes it to heart" is unclear. The NAB translates that phrase as, "with no one giving it a thought."

■ **Isaiah 57:2.** The meaning of this verse is not clear. The thought seems to be that the righteous die peacefully, in contrast to the wicked, on whom judgment is announced (vv. 3-13).

■ **Isaiah 57:5.** Groves of trees were favored by devotees of fertility cults. Valleys were favored by worshipers of underworld deities.

■ **Isaiah 57:7-8.** These verses refer to cultic practices that involve sexual activity on the part of the worshipers.

■ **Isaiah 57:9.** Molek is likely an underworld deity, as is evident from the reference about descending "to the very realm of the dead."

■ **Isaiah 57:14-21.** The problems of the early postexilic age are in contrast to the expectations of the second Isaiah. Some persons apparently wonder if God will be angry forever. God responds, "No, but the fault is yours, not mine. I am always ready to heal the situation."

■ **Isaiah 57:19.** The words, "says the LORD," are a standard conclusion to a prophetic speech (as in 45:13; 54:10, 17; 65:25; 66:9). So verses 20-21 are probably a later addition.

■ **Isaiah 58:1-14.** The problems of the recently reestablished community have led to fasting, a sign of the people's religious intentions. Yet some of their actions contradict their religious understanding and devotion. The prophet now must redefine fasting. Fasting is not merely an inner contrition. Fasting is also an external activity in response to others.

■ **Isaiah 58:4.** The setting for this service is a public, liturgical event. The prophet uses this event as an occasion to speak.

■ **Isaiah 58:6.** The expression "to set the oppressed free" may have reminded the audience of their recent exile, where they were not allowed to go "free" (45:13). The prophet is suggesting that the exiles should have learned from experience.

■ **Isaiah 58:12.** Here is evidence that the locale of the prophet and his audience is no longer Babylon (as it was in chaps. 40–55), but Jerusalem. The city is still in ruins, and the Temple is not yet rebuilt.

■ **Isaiah 58:13-14.** These verses return to the Sabbath theme, with which the words of the third Isaiah began (56:1-2). This pattern suggests that chapters 56–58 may have once been an independent unit.

■ **Isaiah 59:1-21.** The prophet apparently has heard a charge against God that has been expressed by the community or by its leaders. (58:3; 56:3). The prophet dismisses this charge in verse 1. He then lays out a counter-charge (vv. 2-8). In acknowledgment of the rightness of his accusations, a public response, in the form of a first-person lament, has been placed after the counter-charge (vv. 9-15). In response to contriteness, God is then prepared to act (vv. 15-21).

■ **Isaiah 59:6.** The first use of the word "their" alludes to the spider of verse 5. The second use refers to people.

■ **Isaiah 59:9.** The "so" that begins a public response refers to the charges in the previous verses.

■ **Isaiah 59:13-20.** The transition is abrupt. The prophet's disciples have used a speech about God's revenge against the wicked as a response to the public lament in verses 9-15. At first glance, the speech sounds like an announcement that God is about to engage in war to defend Judah from external enemies, or free the exiles from Babylonia. Note the expressions, "his enemies" and "the islands" (v. 18); "from the west . . . [to] the rising of the sun" (v. 19); "to Zion" (v. 20). External enemies now have been replaced by unjust ones from within. The new application is accomplished by the addition of the two small phrases "that there was no justice" (v. 15) and "to those in Jacob who repent of their sins" (v. 20).

■ **Isaiah 59:16.** "There was no one" is an abbreviated expression. The meaning would be clearer if the verse read "There was no one to give assistance."

DIMENSION THREE: WHAT DOES THE BIBLE MEAN TO ME?

Isaiah 56:1-2; 58:13-14—The Sabbath

The importance of this weekly observance in the thought of the prophet is evident. Advice concerning the Sabbath opens the collection. The Sabbath is referred to in other places as well.

Israel's legal tradition traced the roots of this observance back to at least the time of Moses. Moses included the Sabbath among ten essential responses (the Ten Commandments) to God's gracious actions (Exodus 20:1-17). While the Sabbath was observed by succeeding generations (Amos 8:5); it does not seem to have had a predominant role in the calendar. Only at the time of the Exile does the Sabbath rise to a position of importance in religious life. The Sabbath was regarded as of such importance, apparently, that even God was thought to observe it (Genesis 2:4)!

Why do you think the Sabbath suddenly became an item of such importance? Why would other, traditional means of celebrating God have diminished in importance during the Exile? What is the basic function of this observance? Why do you think Sabbath observance is important for the church now?

Isaiah 56:3-8—An Enduring Memorial

The prophet examines the problem of community membership, and concludes that it is open to any who love the Lord (v. 6). This was a bold idea to propose, since it rejects prior sacred tradition (Deuteronomy 23:1-8). The prophet is apparently so impressed by the devotion of some foreigners, something that the second Isaiah had anticipated (45:22-23), that he now announces that a new era has begun.

The prophet then moves from this brief discussion of requirements for membership to a blessing that may come to those who are members of the community. He concentrates on the eunuch, who, because of his physical limitations, cannot produce offspring. The duties of children (and especially the oldest male) included: (1) preserving their parents' allotment of land, (2) carrying on the faith they had learned from their parents, and (3) calling the parents' names at the tomb when offerings were brought so that the parents would be remembered. However, the eunuch cannot be remembered in these ways.

Our feeling of helplessness in the face of death, along with the awareness of the negation it brings, unites us with these ancient people. How do modern persons try to come to terms with their mortality? What are our own means of coping with death? What response to this biological reality does the prophet propose? What meaning does that response have for us today?

*See, I will create new heavens and a new earth. / The former
things will not be remembered. (65:17)*

13

VISION OF
A NEW
JERUSALEM
Isaiah 60–66

DIMENSION ONE:
WHAT DOES THE BIBLE SAY?

Answer these questions by reading Isaiah 60

1. Who does this chapter address? (60:10-11, 14)

2. What are the people who were in exile doing? (60:4)

3. How does the prophet describe the restored community?
   (60:11, 17, 21)

Answer these questions by reading Isaiah 61

4. Has the restoration of the city begun yet? (61:4)

5. What will be the attitude of foreigners toward the
   community? (61:6)

6. What is the response of the community to this proposed new status? (61:10)

Answer this question by reading Isaiah 62

7. What is the new relationship between God and the people compared to? (62:4-5)

Answer these questions by reading Isaiah 63

8. What event from the past is the prophet citing? (63:11-12)

9. What suggests that a group within the community is praying, rather than the entire group? (63:16)

10. What tragedy has befallen the sanctuary? (63:18)

Answer these questions by reading Isaiah 64

11. To what do the speakers attribute their present misfortunes? (64:5-6)

12. What does the speaker ask for? (64:8-9)

Answer these questions by reading Isaiah 65

13. How did Judah respond to God's presence? (65:1-2)

14. Who is God going to save? (65:8-9)

15. Although the prophet speaks of new heavens and a new earth, what is his real concern? (65:17-18)

Answer these questions by reading Isaiah 66

16. What evidence is there of divisiveness within the community? (66:5)

17. How have skeptics described the half-finished restoration of Jerusalem? (66:9)

18. How will God treat Jerusalem? (66:12-13)

19. Why are messengers sent to the nations? (66:19)

DIMENSION TWO: WHAT DOES THE BIBLE MEAN?

■ **Background.** Chapters 56–66 are among the most controversial and difficult chapters in the entire Book of Isaiah. Modern interpreters disagree about how many authors there are, how many units of speech there are, and about the range of dates involved (suggestions range from the late sixth to the early second centuries BC).
■ **Isaiah 60–62.** These chapters, continuing the enthusiasm and optimism that characterized chapters 40–55, are sometimes attributed to the second Isaiah. Usually they are thought to be the earliest speeches of the third Isaiah. They

differ only slightly from the speeches of Second Isaiah. They differ more from the chapters that follow them.

■ **Isaiah 60.** God is the speaker throughout, even when we see references in the third person (the word *his* in v. 2). Note the first-person references in verses 7, 10, 15, 17, and especially 22. (This sets the chapter apart from chap. 61, where the prophet speaks of himself). The audience seems to be in Jerusalem and not in Babylonia, as they were in chapters 40–55.

■ **Isaiah 60:19-20.** The writer of Revelation made use of these ideas at 21:3 and 22:5.

■ **Isaiah 61:1-11.** In verses 1-3, the prophet states his self-understanding. Verses 4-9 reveal what God's activity will mean for the audience. The congregation then responds to God's message (vv. 10-11).

■ **Isaiah 61:3.** Although this speech may have been delivered soon after the return of the exiles (539 BC), despair already has begun. The task of restoration and the lack of resources are overwhelming. The expression "in Zion" fixes the prophet's location.

■ **Isaiah 61:11.** Lest the audience expect overnight results, the prophet compares restoration to the growth of nature. Results are sure, but the process has its own schedule.

■ **Isaiah 62.** The prophet's insistent tone may suggest that time has passed since his announcements in chapters 60–61.

■ **Isaiah 62:2.** A new name signals a new beginning, as when Jacob's name is changed to Israel (Genesis 35:10). The new names are given in verse 4.

■ **Isaiah 62:4.** *Deserted* was used to describe the community previously (54:6; 60:15; see also Jeremiah 4:29). *Desolate* was also a description of Judah (1:7; 6:11; Jeremiah 4:27; 6:8). The analogy of marriage and divorce to describe God's relationship to the people is common in the prophets (50:1; 54:5).

■ **Isaiah 62:8.** These verses reverse the curse that prophets sometimes announced (Micah 6:15).

■ **Isaiah 62:10-12.** The speaker now imitates the style and vocabulary of the second Isaiah at 40:3-4, 9-10.

■ **Isaiah 63:1-6.** The question "Who is this coming?" is one a sentry would ask. The word *Edom* is probably used here as a symbol for all enemies of the community.

■ **Isaiah 63:7–64:12.** Before addressing God about the problems of the present at verse 15, the speaker recites evidence of God's willingness to act in the past (63:7-14). This recitation of the past gives hope in the present. Following the plea for help is a confession of sin (64:5-7), an expression of confidence (64:8), and a resumption of the plea (64:9-12).

■ **Isaiah 63:7-14.** This section of the prayer (whether recited by the prophet or the community is not clear) is similar to Psalm 44. It may be a familiar piece of liturgy rather than a composition by the prophet.

■ **Isaiah 63:10.** This verse apparently refers to the Exile.

■ **Isaiah 63:16.** The expression "though Abraham does not know us / or Israel acknowledge us" is obscure. Some interpreters think the prophet's followers lament that the priestly leaders of Judah do not share their point of view. The expressions may mean that the community, in its struggles, no longer seems to share in the promises made to Abraham and Israel (Jacob). The "fathers" of the community, here treated as if they are still present, do not favor the community.

■ **Isaiah 63:18.** Does this verse refer to the destruction of the Temple in 587 BC at the hands of the Babylonians? Or does it refer to a brief period in the immediate past when the prophet's community had control of liturgical leadership? This period ended when the Zadokite/Aaronite priests came to power.

■ **Isaiah 64:1.** The prophet here refers to stories of God's past appearances (Exodus 19:16-18; Psalm 18:7-9).

■ **Isaiah 64:11.** The reference to the burned Temple as if it were a recent event has caused some interpreters to suggest that 63:7–64:12 was composed by Judeans who remained behind when the exiles were taken away. If so, the passage would be earlier than the time of the third Isaiah.

■ **Isaiah 65:1-25.** This chapter illustrates well how the shape of prophetic preaching has changed. The message of the preexilic prophets was almost entirely negative. The message of the exilic Second Isaiah was almost entirely positive in accordance with the needs of the situation. Now we find a mixture of doom and salvation.

The Judeans no longer agree in their attitude toward God. Some are responsive, some are not. It would do no good to condemn the whole for the sake of the wicked. Such an approach would not now be effective. Moreover, the second Isaiah had renounced such an approach in God's name (54:7-10). So, following a word of condemnation for some (65:1-7) is a statement of distinction (v. 8), then a mixture of positive and negative prophecies (vv. 9-16). Finally, the prophet shifts from moral comparisons to comparing the present and the future (vv. 17-25).

■ **Isaiah 65:4.** Consulting the spirits of the dead about the future was well known in the ancient Near East (1 Samuel 28).

■ **Isaiah 65:11.** *Fortune* and *Destiny* are titles of deities.

■ **Isaiah 65:17-25.** This powerful vision of a renewed world is made up of quotations and allusions to earlier sayings in the Book of Isaiah.

■ **Isaiah 65:1-19.** The idea here is picked up from 35:10; 51:11. The idea will, in turn, inspire the author of Revelation 21:1-4.

■ **Isaiah 65:25.** This verse is a close paraphrase of 11:6-9.

■ **Isaiah 66:1-14.** This chapter is one of the most difficult in Isaiah in terms of the relationship of its various topics. Has it as many as seven separate units or as few as one? The meaning changes according to how verses are grouped together.

■ **Isaiah 66:1-2.** (1) Is this speech against temple building as such? (2) Does it oppose only the present plans, which were different from the Temple that was destroyed? (3) Does the speech oppose only the claim that God's blessing depends on completion of the Temple (as the contemporary prophet

Haggai proclaimed in 2:18-19)? (4) Is this speech traditional praise of God as one whose glory no temple can contain (as in 1 Kings 8:27)? Verse 2b (if it is an original continuation of verses 1-2a) suggests the third of these options.

■ **Isaiah 66:3-4.** The grammar of verse 3a is obscure. Perhaps a comparison is being made, stating that all sacrificial acts are forbidden (see option 1 above). This verse may be condemning both legitimate and illegitimate cultic acts. The CEV uses the translation, "You sacrifice oxen to me, / and you commit murder." The latter possibility is more likely, in view of criticism of strange cultic practices in 65:3-5 and 66:17 (all three verses refer to pigs as sacrificial animals).

■ **Isaiah 66:5.** This verse could be an independent pronouncement. Or it could continue a speech that began in verse 1, so that "you who tremble at his word" would refer to the same groups as does verse 2 ("tremble at my word"). The prophet's own community has been hated and cast out by the predominant priestly leadership. This interpretation would mean that those who do the terrible things in verse 3 are not merely individuals here and there, but the official leadership in the Temple. Their activities may be described in exaggerated terms. Even if the verse is an independent statement, the community is deeply divided over religious matters, and the prophet's point of view is not the official one.

■ **Isaiah 66:18-23.** The divisiveness within the community that chapters 63–66 have alluded to is now balanced with a vision of a united community. This passage is similar in spirit to chapters 60–62, and to the ideas of the second Isaiah. In fact, it may have been intended to return to a theme that began the book: the "all the nations" will come "to my holy mountain" (66:20), just as in 2:2, "all the nations will stream to it."

■ **Isaiah 66:22-23.** The permanence of the new situation is stressed for those who might wonder if the problems of the past could return. (The same point was made by the second Isaiah at 54:9-10; 51:6).

■ **Isaiah 66:24.** The permanence of the salvation that verses 22-23 describe is not paralleled by a statement of the permanent demise of human rebelliousness. The memory of the terrible cost of human pride will not be forgotten. The prophet puts this graphically; the corpses will be a perpetual reminder. This verse is not a reference to punishment in hell, which is a later concept.

DIMENSION THREE: WHAT DOES THE BIBLE MEAN TO ME?

Isaiah 65:25—The Apocalyptic Outlook

The prophet was troubled by tensions in the community and opposition by neighbors. He could not find hope in the framework of ordinary history. The optimism of chapters 60–62 fades. The appeal to the community to obey and reform itself is replaced by announcements of destruction. An appeal is made for a purge of the world that will produce an unending utopia. This point of view, arising from the situation of the third Isaiah, contrasts with the optimism we find in the second Isaiah.

Compare the outlook of the third Isaiah with that of the first Isaiah (see esp. chaps. 1–39). Consider, for example, the nearly identical sayings that are found at 65:25 and 11:6-9. How do their expectations for the future differ? What accounts for that difference? Why might each prophet have refused to adopt the stance of the other? When is an apocalyptic stance helpful to the community and faithful to God? What about apocalyptic announcements in the present? When are these announcements helpful? When are they harmful?

Isaiah 65:1-7—What Is God Really Like?

Christians will occasionally portray the God of ancient Israel and the Old Testament as aloof and judgmental. The God of Jesus is portrayed as near, forgiving, and loving. Discuss this attitude in light of Isaiah 65:1-7.

Isaiah 65:17-25—Utopia

The ideal future as outlined in 65:17-25 differs from later portraits of the age to come. Compare these verses with Revelation 21:1-4, and note any differences. Something the writer of Revelation regards as an absolute evil, to be abolished forever, the third Isaiah does not regard as a problem.

Why do you think death came to be seen as a theological problem? Why was it not a matter of great concern to the third Isaiah or any of his predecessors in the Old Testament? What are your own personal feelings about mortality?

About the Writer

Dr. Lloyd Bailey served as a professor of Old Testament studies at Duke University Divinity School and an ordained elder in the Western North Carolina Conference of The United Methodist Church.